Green Smoothies for Kids

Teach Your
Children
to Enjoy
Healthy
Eating

BY
SIMONE
MCGRATH

Skyhorse Publishing

Skyhorse Publishing books may be purchased in bulk at special discounts for sales promotion, corporate gifts, fund-raising, or educational purposes. Special editions can also be created to specifications. For details, contact the Special Sales Department, Skyhorse Publishing, 307 West 36th Street, 11th Floor, New York, NY 10018 or info@skyhorsepublishing.com.

Skyhorse® and Skyhorse Publishing® are registered trademarks of Skyhorse Publishing, Inc.®, a Delaware corporation.

Visit our website at www.skyhorsepublishing.com.

10 9 8 7 6 5 4 3 2 1

Library of Congress Cataloging-in-Publication Data is available on file.

Cover design by Laura Klynstra
Cover photo credit: istock.com
Interior photo credits: istock.com and bigstockphoto.com

Print ISBN: 978-1-5107-0408-4
Ebook ISBN: 978-1-5107-0409-1

Printed in China

Disclaimer: This book is not meant to be used to diagnose or treat any medical condition. For diagnosis or treatment of any medical condition, consult a physician. Always consult a physician before starting a new diet or wellness program.

Table of Contents

Introduction

Frustrated moms of the world unite!

We all know how important a diet rich in fresh fruits and vegetables is for our kids. Getting a willful child to eat them is, of course, another story!

Children seem to be born with a built-in mechanism that makes them want to run screaming from vegetables, especially the green kind. Whether they express their displeasure by being sullen or throwing a tantrum, we sit at the dinner table bargaining and cajoling, determined to get some broccoli down the gullets of our kids, who sit steadfast in their resolve to not allow any of it past their tightly clamped lips.

Eventually we bribe them: "If you eat your veggies, then you can have a candy." This negates the health benefits of the veggies, and does not help to engender good eating habits and food choices. Veggies become viewed as a means to an end, as a way to get something they want. Sometimes we simply give up and leave the veggies out because we're tired at the end of a long day, and few of us have the energy to argue and stick to our good intentions of getting our kids to eat some vegetables, no matter what.

Unfortunately, the above scenarios are all steeped in negativity and set up an adversarial relationship with healthy food and healthy living, which only becomes more entrenched as the child gets older. This cycle of negativity becomes harder to break, and people become comfortable with their unhealthy way of life. The thing that falls by the wayside is the thing that we should be striving to achieve against all else, and that is to teach our children to enjoy eating healthy foods and to make healthy food choices willingly. When they do it as second nature it becomes their lifestyle, and that above all else is the most important gift we can give our children.

It all sounds great on paper, doesn't it? But how do you implement it in real life, when you're sitting across the table stuck in a staring match with your four-year-old over a plate of spinach?

It's really easy—toss the spinach! Yes, that's right, you read it correctly. Toss it . . . right into the blender, along with an apple, half a banana, and finish it off with a splash of almond milk for good measure. Blitz it, pour it, stick in a straw, and your kids should be good to go.

Green smoothies are the way forward. You need them in your life. Your kids will love them, and I'm here to tell you how to do it right and nip that healthy food rebellion in the bud!

So, put your feet up and get reading. A healthy family is on the horizon!

The Importance of Fruits and Vegetables

We've all heard the health experts and doctors expounding the virtues of a diet rich in fruits and vegetables, but what exactly is it about these food groups that makes them so special?

   Certainly everyone can benefit from eating fruits and vegetables, but for children getting enough of the right kinds of fruits and vegetables into their diet is essential for their growing bodies. Fruits and vegetables contain vital nutrients that feed growing and developing bodies, and a lack of these nutrients can drastically hinder your child's physical and mental development.

Fruits and vegetables are loaded with vitamins, most notably A, C, and K. In addition, they are a source of folic acid, potassium, and other trace minerals. They're one of the healthiest sources of carbohydrates around, with tons of dietary fiber. And if that wasn't enough, some vegetables even contain protein.

Fruits and vegetables are also an important source of phytochemicals, which are instrumental in the prevention of chronic diseases, such as cancer, heart disease, gastric issues, high blood pressure, and diabetes.

Obesity is on the rise worldwide. No longer is being overweight just a problem of middle age. More and more children are showing signs of obesity every year. Why? Well, it's quite simple: they don't eat enough (if any) fruits and vegetables. We live in a society of fast food, where everything is packaged for our convenience, but what we trade for convenience is our health. We overeat yet we're undernourished—this is largely because we eat foods that are calorie dense but lacking in wholesome nutrition. These foods are full of sugar, fat, chemicals, and empty calories. We need to swap this kind of eating for a high-quality diet, ideally one that is largely plant based with good sources of protein as well. In a nutshell, we need to eat more fruits and vegetables to get ourselves back to a healthy state.

In addition, illness in general is on the rise. People are sicker, they take longer to heal, and the easiest thing they can do to help prevent sickness is to eat more fruits and vegetables, since they help boost the immune system. When your immune system is strong it can fight off invasions from foreign elements. However, an army is only as strong as its soldiers, and your immune system can only be effective in keeping germs at bay if you're strong at a cellular level.

It is recommended that we consume, on average, two and a half cups of fresh fruit and two and a half cups of fresh vegetables per day. This amount fluctuates slightly depending on your age and activity level, but on average we don't consume nearly that much per day in our modern lives. Many people lament that it's too much, and they already feel like they're eating "tons" of fruit and vegetables without coming close to the recommended amount. To an extent this is true.

That's why green smoothies are, without a doubt, the way forward. You can get your entire daily allowance of fruits and vegetables in one glass, once a day. What could be easier?

On the following pages, I provide you with the means to better health, and it should take no longer than ten minutes to make a green smoothie, drink it, and clean up afterwards. I think even the busiest of parents can find ten minutes a day to dedicate to their children's health. This book provides you with everything you need to start your children on their green smoothie journey!

Green Ingredients and Their Benefits

So, what's the fuss about all things green? Take a look at what these green ingredients have to offer in the way of nutrition and prepare to be amazed.

Avocado: Not only are avocados delicious, with a creamy texture and simple flavor, but they're also one of the healthiest foods out there. Avocados contain more than 25 essential nutrients, some of the major ones being copper, iron, potassium, folic acid, magnesium, and phosphorus, as well as vitamins A, B, C, E, and K. And if that wasn't enough, they also contain protein, fiber and phytochemicals. Avocados are classified as "healthy fats," so they help to keep your heart healthy. They're

also instrumental in lowering cholesterol levels in the blood. The effects of lower cholesterol can be observed after just a week of including avocados in your diet—that's amazing! The potassium in avocados helps to keep blood pressure levels stable, and they contain anti-inflammatory properties.

Avocados contain carotenoid lutein, which helps to keep your eyes healthy and prevents age–related degeneration of vision. They keep blood sugar levels stable, and, due to all their fiber, they can also help to reverse insulin resistance because they contain monounsaturated fats. This plays a role in stabilizing blood sugar levels. In addition, they're packed full of powerful antioxidants that fight free radicals, and they have been shown to play a role in preventing certain cancers. Avocados help bolster the immune system and keep the nervous system running in peak condition. It has even been shown that avocados can actually help to facilitate the absorption of other nutrients in the body. The oils in avocados are beneficial for skin health, because they nourish the skin and make it glow. Avocados are an incredibly heathy source of calories, and including them in your green smoothies is highly recommended.

Broccoli: Broccoli has an extensive list of health benefits. Not only is it packed full of nutrients, but it also has numerous therapeutic qualities. Broccoli is a source of both soluble and insoluble fiber and contains an impressive amount of vitamin C, which is useful in strengthening immunity and helps the body fight off disease-causing germs. Additionally, broccoli is loaded with vitamins A, K, and B complex, and contains high levels of iron, phosphorus, folic acid, and zinc. It is also a rich source of antioxidants and phytonutrients, which are instrumental in the prevention of more serious diseases, such as diabetes, cancer, and heart disease. It's an important source of calcium too, which is especially beneficial to people who don't eat dairy products.

Research has revealed that broccoli may be useful in protecting you against a number of other health complaints. Broccoli contains a compound that can prevent certain enzymes from destroying cartilage, thus preventing the inflammation that is associated with osteoporosis. Eating broccoli on a regular basis helps to protect the blood vessels in the heart, strengthening them and eliminating the molecules that cause heart damage.

It is highly recommended to eat broccoli raw to gain the maximum benefit from this delicious vegetable. Cooking changes some of the compounds in the vegetable, rendering many of these health benefits useless. What better way to eat raw broccoli than in your green smoothie? Yum!

Celery: Celery is one of the most underrated green vegetables ever! Research has shown that this unassuming plant contains no fewer than eight cancer-fighting compounds. Not content with merely fighting cancer, celery is a nutritional bomb just waiting to explode. Full of vitamins A, B1, B2, B6, and C, it also contains potassium, calcium, magnesium, iron, folate,

sodium, phosphorus, and a host of different amino acids. The vitamin A helps protect your eyes and plays an important role in preventing vision deterioration. Natural, organic sodium is found in celery, but don't confuse this with the sodium that does your body damage. The sodium in celery is safe to consume; in fact, the body actually needs it.

Some of the other amazing health benefits of celery include lowering blood pressure, stabilizing the body's pH, replenishing electrolytes, and rehydrating the body after a workout. It does all this through its rich supply of minerals. Celery is also very effective at lowering cholesterol levels and relieving constipation. A diuretic, it is effective at ridding the body of excess fluid. During this flushing of the system, harmful toxins are expelled from the body, which helps to keep the kidneys functioning optimally.

Celery is a natural anti-inflammatory agent and is effective in relieving the discomfort associated with painful conditions like arthritis, bronchitis, and asthma. Drinking celery juice in your green smoothie will help to soothe frazzled nerves and calm you down, making it a good choice for insomniacs and children who lead a hectic lifestyle.

Cucumber: For such an unassuming vegetable, the cucumber packs a hefty nutritional punch. You've no doubt heard the phrase "cool as a cucumber." Cucumbers are 95 percent water, so they fight the heat from the inside, and on a hot day eating cucumbers will bring down your body temperature. For instant relief from a sunburn, just apply cucumber slices. Completely hydrating, if you don't get your eight-glass-a-day quota of water, simply munch on a delicious, juicy cucumber. The high water content makes cucumbers a natural detoxifyng agent, literally flushing toxins and waste out of your body. Cucumber also adds a boost of vitamins A, B, C, and D, which helps keep immunity levels high, keeps skin glowing, and provides a shot of energy. The minerals in cucumbers that are beneficial to your skin are silicon, folate, calcium, magnesium, and potassium.

Cucumbers not only aid digestion and help lower blood pressure, but they also contain some cancer-fighting compounds and are an effective means of kidney stone prevention. They are a good choice for diabetics, since they contain a specific hormone that is needed by the pancreas to make insulin. Cucumbers help to keep cholesterol levels down. In addition, the phytochemicals in cucumbers kill off the bacteria that cause bad breath, so they help prevent halitosis.

Kale: Heralded as "the queen of greens," this powerhouse vegetable is worth its nutritional weight in gold! Kale is full of fiber, which aids digestion, and it's high in iron, folate, and magnesium, and is especially high in vitamin K, which is essential for cancer prevention, bone health and blood clotting. It also contains high levels of vitamins A and C, which helps to fight off infection, boosts immunity, keeps your metabolism functioning properly, and supports hydration.

Kale is packed full of a range of powerful antioxidants that protect against free radical damage in the body. It helps to lower cholesterol levels, which is great for cardiovascular health, and it has powerful anti-inflammatory properties. It is also rich in omega-3 fatty acids, which help in the fight against autoimmune disorders.

Although a significant percentage of the calories in kale come from protein, it contains so few calories by volume that it makes it an impractical source to meet the body's protein needs.

Kale nourishes the skin and contains more calcium than milk, which keeps bones strong and healthy. The fiber in kale binds to toxins and helps clear them out of the body, helping to keep the liver healthy. Kale is, without a doubt, a vital green to include in your daily diet.

Mint: Fresh herbs are often overlooked as part of a healthy diet, with preference usually given to fruits and vegetables, but herbs are a vital part of any healthy eating plan because they contain an impressive list of health benefits. Mint is far more than a breath freshener! It has one of the highest antioxidant levels of all foods—pretty impressive for just a few green leaves. In addition, mint contains vitamins A and C, as well as small amounts of calcium, iron, fiber, phosphorus, potassium, and magnesium.

Mint plays a role in relieving the symptoms of seasonal allergies when consumed on a regular basis. It is also an anti-inflammatory agent. Mint is great for treating some symptoms of the common cold. It relieves a sore throat when infused into water, and it's a natural decongestant that breaks up mucous. Mint eases digestion by improving the flow of bile through the stomach and relaxing the muscles in the digestive tract, and it's very effective in treating indigestion or an upset tummy.

Parsley: Parsley is more than just a simple garnish; it contains a lion's share in terms of what it can offer your body. This herb is a cancer-fighting giant and has been labeled as a chemoprotective food because it contains a number of compounds that not only inhibit the growth of tumors and neutralize carcinogens, but it also contains an arsenal of antioxidants that protect against free radical damage and oxidative stress in the cells of the body.

There are compounds in parsley that are important in the metabolism of carbohydrates, and it is an anti-inflammatory agent, which fights against degenerative diseases, such as osteoarthritis and rheumatoid arthritis, and provides relief from joint aches and pains. Parsley is rich in vitamins A and C, which serve to strengthen the body's immune responses to infection. It is also rich in folate, which is an instrumental substance in heart health, as well as containing a rich supply of folic acid, which invigorates the heart. Regular consumption of parsley will help to keep cardiovascular diseases at bay and help to control blood pressure.

Parsley contains a generous dose of vitamin K, which is essential for strong bones. Vitamin K prevents calcium from building up in our tissues, which is a leading cause of strokes and cardiovascular disease. Vitamin K is also necessary for the health of the nervous system. It is involved in the synthesis of specific fats needed to maintain the myelin sheath, the insulator that surrounds our nerves. When the myelin sheath is damaged, the transmission of nerve impulses through the nervous system is hindered, so messages may be unable to travel from the brain to other parts of the body.

Romaine lettuce:
The mild flavor of romaine lettuce makes it one of the most perfect greens to include in green smoothies for kids, as they are not likely to even know it's there. It's a good source of fiber, which helps keep the digestive system in peak condition. Any fiber that is not fully digested will help to remove waste and toxins from the digestive tract. Furthermore, diets high in fiber have been shown to reduce the risk of developing diabetes and heart disease.

Romaine lettuce has a high level of vitamin C, helping to keep the heart healthy and boosting immunity. Vitamin C also helps to keep cholesterol from clinging to the blood vessel walls. It's rich in vitamin K, which helps blood clot and keeps bones strong. The potassium in romaine lettuce is essential for maintaining muscle strength. In addition, romaine lettuce is a complete protein, meaning it contains all the essential amino acids your body needs. It is also rich in calcium, copper, zinc, manganese, magnesium, selenium, potassium, phosphorus, omega–3, iron, B vitamins, beta-carotene, and water.

Spinach: Popeye had the right idea! This superfood is jammed full of nutrients, while still managing to be low in calories. Spinach provides high levels of iron and protein and is rich in vitamins and minerals. It is good for the skin, hair, and nails. It also plays a very important role in bone health, helps to lower blood pressure, and reduces the risk of developing asthma as well as cancer. It is good for diabetics, as it helps keep blood glucose levels stable

and prevents the sugar spikes that are characteristic of the disease. Spinach is a good nondairy source of calcium, which is important for those with dairy allergies.

Spinach is a great source of magnesium, which plays a role in many chemical reactions in the body and is instrumental in providing the body with energy and keeping the nerves, heart, and muscles functioning properly, keeping blood pressure in check and the immune system at its peak.

Spinach is rich in vitamins A, C, and K, as well as phosphorus, potassium, zinc, selenium, beta-carotene, thiamine, and fiber. Fiber is good for the digestive system, prevents constipation, and keeps you feeling full longer. The generous amount of vitamin K is also responsible for keeping the brain and nervous system healthy. Spinach is full of antioxidants and phytonutrients and has anti-inflammatory properties. It is one of the most unassuming vegetables to toss into a green smoothie as it has a mild taste that belies its powerful effects. Without a doubt, spinach should be included in your daily diet!

Spirulina: Spirulina is a natural algae that is incredibly high in protein as well as many vitamins and minerals. It's a complete food source. It can be taken as a supplement and can help prevent some health issues, such as obesity, cancer, diabetes, and allergies. Spirulina contains more than 100 different kinds of nutrients—more than any other food source in the world. Spirulina also contains the full range of B complex vitamins, vitamin E, and beta-carotene, as well as iron, phosphorus, chromium, copper, manganese, selenium, potassium, calcium, magnesium, and zinc. In addition, spirulina contains antioxidants and chlorophyll, which help purify the blood and boost immunity.

Spirulina even provides the body with some protein; spirulina is 60 percent protein! This makes it an excellent green smoothie ingredient for children who struggle to consume their daily protein requirements from other sources. It's also a fantastic protein source for vegetarians, who may lack certain amino acids that are necessary for normal metabolic processes within the body due to their embargo on animal meat. Amino acids are helpful in protecting against heart disease. All these substances are hugely beneficial to your overall health.

Spirulina also plays a role in boosting energy and keeping weight stable. It's an important supplement in lowering cholesterol levels—another important role in keeping the heart healthy. Spirulina is a potent antioxidant, which strengthens the immune system. It helps to rev up metabolism, reduce inflammation, improve eyesight, and strengthen teeth and bones. It also contains omega-3, 6, and 9 fatty acids and is especially high in omega-3s.

After reading these unbelievable health benefits, there can be no doubt left in your mind that including greens is vitally important to your children's continued good health. The ingredients speak for themselves.

Health Benefits of Green Smoothies

What is a green smoothie?

A green smoothie is a smoothie that contains one or more green ingredients. It doesn't necessarily have to be green in color. What makes green smoothies so great is that they are immediately absorbed by the body because everything is in its liquid form. Blending the greens liquefies the fibers and makes the nutrients much easier for little bodies to absorb. Greens can be tough on a young child's digestive system; greens in liquid form are easier to digest. Giving your little one a green smoothie a day is an easy way to ensure they get enough greens into their daily diet and, therefore, all of the beneficial nutrients.

Health benefits of green smoothies:

Have a look at this impressive list of health benefits that your children can enjoy simply by including one green smoothie per day in their diet. The more you include the greater the benefits for your children.

1. First, and most importantly, green smoothies are a source of pure nutrition. Greens in any form are great for the body, but chewing them doesn't provide the same level of nutrition that blitzing them does. When you chew greens it doesn't release all of the goodness into your body. When you pulverize them in a blender, the cell membranes are ruptured, and all the nutrients are released to nourish you completely. In their liquid form, the absorption of nutrients begins in the mouth, and you get the maximum benefit from all of the vitamins and minerals. Which vitamins and minerals you get depends on which fruits and vegetables you include, so it's recommended that you include the rainbow. The greater the color and variety of fruits and vegetables you include, the greater the nutritional benefits. Try to include fruits and vegetables of every color, as each group includes a different set of vitamins and minerals.

2. Greens are a great source of nondairy calcium. For children with dairy allergies, who can't get the required calcium intake from milk and milk products, upping their leafy green intake ensures that they will get their daily requirement of calcium without upsetting their allergies. Calcium strengthens bones and teeth and is vital for growing children.

3. Green smoothies are a better option than fresh fruit and vegetable juices. Not only is juicing time consuming and messy, but you only extract the juice and discard the pulp. All the fiber is in the pulp, and fiber is important for digestion. With smoothies you blitz the whole fruit or vegetable, so all the goodness and fiber are included.

4. Most parents battle to get their kids to eat the required number of fruit and vegetable servings per day. A green smoothie is a great way to get all the servings into one glass. For children who don't like to eat greens, including them in a green smoothie helps mask the taste, as the fruit sweetens them up, making them more palatable for kids.

5. Many children don't get the required vitamin intake from food. Drinking green smoothies can help reach that requirement and could eliminate the need for multivitamins, saving you money. In addition, green smoothies are incredibly versatile—change recipes to suit your tastes by leaving out what you don't like and adding in favored ingredients. It's as simple as that!

6. The combination of fruits and vegetables provides a lasting source of energy. Fruits especially have a high sugar content, so eating them alone gives you an initial burst of energy, but it is not sustained. As a result, even a diet high in fruits can make blood sugar levels dip and spike erratically. Combining fruits and vegetables in a green smoothie helps balance things out and stabilizes blood sugar levels.

7. Green smoothies provide all the nutritional needs without adding calories. By their very nature they are low in calories while still being incredibly filling. The high water and fiber content helps you feel full for a longer period of time. While you don't necessarily want your kids to be dieting, it's nice to know that they can be getting a whole bunch of amazing nutrition without gaining weight. However, if you have a child who needs to be on a calorie-restricted diet, green smoothies are a great way to ensure that they don't miss out on valuable nutrition.

8. Green smoothies are easy on the digestive system, which is good for younger children. Since the ingredients are broken down into their liquid form, it means they're primed for maximum nutrient absorption. Little bodies don't have to work so hard to break down the food in order to extract the nutrients. As an added bonus, green smoothies are a great way to keep your system regular. The added fiber does wonders for children suffering from constipation.

9. Experts recommend drinking six to eight glasses of water per day, but not many of us reach that goal. Children especially fall way below their recommended water intake level. Green smoothies are a great way to add extra water into their diet without them even realizing it. For more adventurous kids, try adding some coconut water or even green tea for an added flavor dimension and nutrient boost.

10. Green smoothies are perfectly portable and can be packed in school lunches or taken to sporting events. Provided they are stored correctly and kept cool, they will keep for at least 24 hours or more.

11. Consuming greens in smoothies may reduce the amount of oil and salt in your children's diet. Think about it, do you try to make greens more appealing by adding cheese sauce, butter, or salt to entice your children to eat them? With green smoothies there is no added sauce, salt, or fats, and the flavor of the greens gets lost in the flavors of the other ingredients. This makes green smoothies an all-around healthier alternative.

12. Green smoothies help provide mental clarity; all the natural goodness literally clears the mind and lifts the fog. Diets containing processed food, junk food, and sugar clog up kids' minds, slowing down their thinking and reactions. With a diet containing more whole foods, children are able to think more clearly, they become more focused, and creativity improves. What better combination of attributes are required for good school performance?

13. The body craves junk food because it provides that initial burst of energy. The more junk you eat, the more your blood sugar level dips and spikes, so the more you crave junk food; it's a vicious cycle. Eating healthy food fills the body with goodness and keeps blood sugar levels more stable. As a result, kids don't need that quick fix of energy, because they're getting long-lasting energy that releases slowly. Green smoothies are a great way to limit children from snacking between meals for this very reason. The fiber helps keep them full longer, so they're able to keep going until their next meal.

14. Experts are always expounding the benefits of a diet rich in fruits and vegetables to help in the prevention of diseases, especially heart disease and cancer. What better way to increase the intake of these vital foods than through a green smoothie? Knowing you're protecting your children's heart and lowering the risk of cancer is an added bonus.

15. Green smoothies are great for the skin. The vitamins help improve overall skin tone and help reduce the appearance of wrinkles. While it's not a concern for kids, I'm sure overworked parents like the idea of fewer wrinkles and a healthy glow. For older kids, green smoothies can help prevent acne breakouts, because they load the body with the vitamins and minerals that are lacking in the diets of many teens today. The skin is the first place where bad eating habits show. If you include green smoothies in your kids' diet on a regular basis, their skin will reap the benefits.

There really is no downside to drinking green smoothies. Go green today!

Stocking Up for Green Smoothies

You should be able to find most green smoothie staples at your local supermarket, but some of the more exotic ingredients may require a trip to a specialty health food store. I recommend buying fresh, organic produce. One of the best places to find this is at a local farmers' market, which can be a lovely outing for the whole family. Since the food there is generally not manufactured for commercial purposes, they are likely to have minimal to no pesticides, chemicals, and hormones. I cannot stress it more that for obvious reasons this is the best way to go for your kids. Having a healthy lifestyle means having a clean lifestyle, and that means avoiding artificial chemicals whenever possible.

At the supermarket you should be able to find all the ingredients you need around the perimeter of the store, where the whole foods are traditionally stocked. So, with a little forward planning you can avoid the aisles with all the contraband (for most kids out of sight, out of mind works wonders), do a quick sweep around the store, and employ some CIA-style distraction techniques as you navigate your children past the candy to the register and exit with your cart full of delicious, wholesome, fresh foods. A good way to get this done with kids in tow is to move through the checkout as quickly as possible—never go to the store during peak times if you can avoid it. That way you can breeze past the sweets stocked near the checkout, pay quickly, and leave. During peak hours, you can stand in line for up to thirty minutes, and that is a recipe for trouble when you have children with you.

This leads to the number one golden rule of green smoothie shopping: Do not shop when your kids are hungry. This is just setting yourself up for failure. Make sure everyone eats a wholesome, nutritious meal before you go to the store. You'll be less likely to cheat, impulse buy, and set in motion the guilt-induced self-flagellation if your hunger is satisfied than if you go to the store ravenously hungry. Even things you wouldn't normally eat seem appealing when you're hungry, and the same is true for children. A nutritious meal or snack beforehand (perfect time for a green smoothie) will ensure that blood sugar levels are stable, so kids (and adults) will be less likely to feel the pull of candy bar cravings.

Another great way to avoid succumbing to the temptation of naughty eats, cheats, and treats is to always be prepared. Plan your green smoothies in advance, write a shopping list and only take enough cash to buy the essentials. Explain to children before you leave the house that you

only have enough money to buy what is on the list and nothing extra. This is a great way to avoid impulse buys and will also help if you are shopping on a budget. Organic green smoothie shopping can be expensive, but doesn't have to break the bank if you plan and budget well, so make sure you shop smart. Look out for specials and bulk buys. When you get home you have two options. One is to wash, chop, and freeze the fresh fruits and veggies until you need them for green smoothies. Freezing them yourself is preferable to buying them frozen. Prepackaged, frozen fruits may be loaded with additional sugar (more about this later), and freezing them yourself guarantees freshness. The second option is to purchase some popsicle molds, then blend up some green smoothies and freeze them in the mold. This way you will have delicious and healthy frozen treats for your kids whenever you need them. Not many children can resist the lure of a popsicle, and they probably won't even question what they're made of, especially if the green smoothies are the purples and reds of traditional popsicles.

Any of the green smoothie recipes in this book can be used to make popsicles, but turn the page for an easy and tasty green smoothie popsicle recipe your kids will love.

Berry Good Popsicles

The coconut milk in these green smoothie popsicles gives these frozen treats a creamy texture and provides a boost of healthy fats for growing bodies. They're sweetened naturally with fruit and have added nutrition provided by some sneaky greens. The kids are going to love them!

Yields: 6 Servings

Ingredients:
- 1 cup coconut milk, unsweetened
- 1 frozen banana, chopped
- 1 cup frozen mixed berries
- ½ cup kale, chopped

Directions:
1. Place all ingredients in a blender and blend until very smooth.
2. Transfer mixture into 6 popsicle molds.
3. Place in the freezer.
4. When they are half frozen, stick a popsicle stick in each one and leave in the freezer until completely frozen.

In terms of the most kid-friendly green smoothie ingredients that you should always have on hand, try to keep your kitchen stocked with the following staples.

Apples: There's a reason for the old adage: "An apple a day keeps the doctor away." It's because they are nothing short of nutritional powerhouses! Green apples contain a host of vital health benefits. First, they are an excellent source of fiber. Fiber is crucial for proper digestion, which not only keeps you regular, but also helps to ward off colon cancer. Due to the high fiber content, green apples keep you feeling full longer, so they help curb your appetite. Green apples help to lower blood pressure and keep blood

sugar levels stable throughout the day. Since they contain carbohydrates, natural sugars, and protein, they're a good source of energy. Green apples are jammed full of an assortment of vitamins and minerals, most notably, vitamins A, B6, and C, and are high in iron, potassium, calcium, magnesium, copper, zinc, manganese, and riboflavin. Green apples also contain antioxidants, which help fight off cancer by preventing the DNA damage done by free radicals. Green apples protect the liver, nourish the skin, and help to keep cholesterol levels in check. They're fantastic for detoxing and cleansing the blood. In addition, they're great for indigestion, because they contain both maleic acid and tartaric acid, which help settle the stomach after a heavy meal.

Containing fiber, vitamins and minerals, apples are good for you from head to toe. As an added bonus, apples are not a seasonal fruit and are available year-round in most places.

Almond milk: Almond milk is a popular substitute for those wishing to avoid dairy and for kids who are intolerant to dairy. It is readily available in most stores, but there are wide variances depending on flavors and brand. However, it can easily be made at home by soaking, grinding, and straining raw almonds. This way you will know exactly what's in it. Almond milk is lower in calories and fat than cow's milk and has the added benefit of not causing any digestive complaints. Homemade plain almond milk can have as few as 30 calories and 2.5 grams of fat per serving, while cow's milk has 120 calories and 5 grams of fat per serving.

Another positive is that because almond milk is not an animal product it contains neither cholesterol nor saturated fat. It can also be stored at room temperature for a few days without spoiling, making it ideal for taking to school, sporting events, and for camping. Almond milk is rich in zinc, potassium, and phosphorus, making it an ideal low-calorie, nutritious green smoothie ingredient. If you have children with nut allergies but don't want to lose that delicious creamy milk texture in their green smoothie, simply substitute coconut milk for almond milk.

Baby spinach and kale: Loaded with vitamins, minerals, and protein, these are the greens you want to start with. Not only are they the richest nutritionally, but they also have the mildest flavor and are the easiest to get kids to accept. Purchase them fresh or dried in powder form, or chop up fresh spinach or kale and freeze in small portions to use as needed.

Berries: The health benefits of berries are second to none. Full of vitamin C, fiber, and antioxidants, they are also a natural source of energy. The antioxidants contained in berries help the body fight oxidative stress caused by free radicals that can lead to many types of illness. Eating a diet rich in antioxidants can help improve all areas of your health and prevent certain diseases. All fruits and vegetables contain antioxidants, but berries are some of the absolute best sources. Choose from the full range of berries and add at least one to every green smoothie. Children love red and purple smoothies, and this is where you are going to get the brightness from. Kids also love the taste, so it's bound to be a winning ingredient.

Freshly squeezed juices: Orange, pineapple, and apple juice are preferred. Squeezing your own juices means you get far more health benefits than you get from store-bought juices. Freshly squeezed juices taste absolutely delicious, so using them as a base for green smoothies takes the flavor up a notch. It's a great idea to start off using these juices for new green smoothie drinkers, since they mask the flavor of the greens and add sweetness.

Grapes: In addition to their awesome taste, grapes offer a range of health benefits that truly up the stakes of any green smoothie. Green grapes are considered to be a healthy source of carbohydrates because they contain fiber as well as essential vitamins, minerals, and electrolytes that promote good health. They help to maintain the proper fluid balance in cells, and the correct acidity levels in blood, and accordingly play a role in peak muscle function. Because of the high levels of electrolytes present in green grapes, they are a good source of replenishment after exercise or exertion. They contain antioxidants, which protect against the free radical damage that may lead to certain cancers, and they also help to protect the heart by reducing inflammation and preventing the formation of blood clots. Rich in vitamins A, C, and K, they are crucial for boosting immunity and helping wounds to heal.

Exciting new research has shown that green grapes cause the blood vessels in the body to dilate, which allows the blood to flow more freely, thus lowering blood pressure and reducing the risk of heart attack. By dilating the blood vessels, it also allows for a higher volume of blood to flow through the vessels at any one time, improving oxygen supply and facilitating the delivery of nutrients to the body. Increased blood flow to the brain means improved mental focus and clarity and improved concentration. Add them as is or freeze them first before adding them to a green smoothie for a thicker texture.

Kiwifruit: Bright green in color, speckled with black seeds, and providing amazing taste, this exotic, unique fruit is a powerhouse of nutrition. These emerald delights add more than just eye candy; they're packed full of vitamins, minerals, and phytochemicals that promote good health. Kiwifruit aids digestion and contains enzymes that help break down proteins. They contain high levels of potassium, which help to counteract the effects of sodium, thereby keeping the body's electrolytes in a state of balance.

Kiwifruit contains a unique combination of powerful antioxidants that help to diminish the effects of oxidative stress and protects the body from free radical damage; this is vital in the prevention of cancer. Kiwifruit has a very high level of vitamin C, which is instrumental in boosting immunity and protecting the body from illness. It's considered to be a "smart carbohydrate," because it has a high fiber content and is low on the glycemic index, which means it does not provide a big blood sugar rush like other fruits do, thus helping to keep blood sugar levels on an even keel. This makes it a great fruit for diabetics. The high levels of fiber help to keep the digestive system functioning regularly and helps ward off intestinal problems, like constipation. Your body eliminates toxins easily through a regular functioning digestive tract, keeping you clean and detoxed and aiding in the prevention of colon cancer.

Kiwifruit has been shown to reduce the occurrence of blood clots, and in this way helps to prevent heart disease. Categorized as an alkaline fruit, they help neutralize the acidic foods we consume and are helpful in maintaining the body's acid/alkaline balance. Kiwifruit also contains a high dose of vitamin E, which is great for the skin. A study has highlighted that these fruits might be able to offer protection against respiratory-related health issues, such as coughing at night, shortness of breath, and wheezing, and have also offered some relief from asthma symptoms. It is believed that the powerful antioxidant content is what offers such protection. Kids love the bright color and great taste, so kiwifruit is a fantastic addition to any green smoothie. Chop them up and add as is or freeze them before adding to a green smoothie for a different texture.

Pears: Another fantastic source of vitamins, minerals, and antioxidants, delicious, juicy pears are essential for optimal health. Green pears are an excellent source of dietary fiber, which is essential for a healthy digestive system. A healthy and regular digestive system goes a long way towards preventing the development of colon cancer. Fiber also helps to bind to any toxins in the gut and effectively eliminate them from the body, as well as acting as a natural laxative. This high level of fiber combined with relatively low calories makes this fruit an excellent means of keeping cholesterol in check and maintaining an optimum overall body weight.

Green pears are rich in vitamins A, C, and B complex, as well as having plenty of phytonutrients and free radical fighting antioxidants. They contain a number of important minerals including potassium, manganese, magnesium, copper, iron, folates, and riboflavin, all of which have specific and vital roles to play in the body. They are also being heralded as being effective in managing diabetes, as well as protecting against cancer and heart disease.

Green pears have been labeled as one of the least allergenic fruits on the planet, which makes them suitable for children with allergies and food intolerances. Another interesting fact: the skin of green pears contains at least three times the level of phytonutrients that is contained in the flesh of the fruit and half of its overall dietary fiber, so whatever you do, don't peel them! Chop them up and add them as is or freeze them first to add a thicker texture.

Tropical fruits: Pineapple, mango, and banana are amazing ingredients, because they're naturally sweet and add a burst of color to green smoothies. They also add a creamy texture and naturally thicken up a green smoothie without having to resort to yogurts and the like. Tropical fruits have quite strong flavors and can mask greens instantly. Chop them up and add them as is or freeze in small portions to use as needed. Using them frozen adds a thick, icy, creamy consistency.

I have no doubt that there are plenty of other ingredients that your kids will love. Have fun experimenting to find their preferred combinations. Once you find their favorites, always make sure your kitchen is stocked and prepared for an imminent green smoothie attack! It's a fun learning curve and a great way to spend some quality time with your kids.

Amazing Additional Ingredients

Once your kids are drinking green smoothies on a regular basis, here are some amazing additional ingredients that you can throw in for an extra health and flavor boost.

Açaí berries: This little known berry is one of the healthiest foods you will ever find and holds its own among the superfood heavyweights. Hailing from the Amazon, this antioxidant rich fruit has been renowned for centuries for its immune-boosting, healing, re-energizing and tasty qualities. Related to cranberries and blueberries, this exotic cousin is well known for fighting the effects of oxidative stress caused by free radical damage. Açaí berries lower cholesterol and provide many other cardiac benefits when consumed on

a regular basis. The walls of the blood vessels relax, which improves overall blood circulation to all areas of the body, thereby reducing blood pressure and helping to prevent blood clots from forming.

Açaí berries help keep weight stable when used as part of a calorie-controlled diet. They also promote healthy skin—by nourishing your insides you project an outward radiant glow. An excellent source of dietary fiber, they're instrumental in optimal digestive health and help remove harmful substances, toxins, and chemicals by detoxing the body and blood.

Açaí berries contain a number of soothing compounds and may help with respiratory irritation. They overhaul your insides at a cellular level by keeping individual cells strong against the invasion of germs, disease, and free radicals. Açaí berries contain high doses of vitamin C, which helps keep the immune system strong. They're also beneficial in preventing the growth of cancerous cells. The phytochemicals that are found inside these berries are believed to stop the process of carcinogenesis at a molecular level.

Açaí has enormous energy-boosting capabilities and is helpful in fighting fatigue and increasing energy and stamina levels. These berries improve mental function by boosting the blood circulation; more blood to the brain means more oxygen, which in turn means better performance. These are an excellent addition to your child's green smoothies, as the health benefits just cannot be beat!

Chia seeds: These very small black seeds come from the *Salvia Hispanica* plant. This is related to the mint plant and grows natively in South America. The Aztecs and Mayans considered the chia seed to be an important food source and prized them for the sustained energy they provided. "Chia" is the Mayan word for "strength."

Loaded with nutrients and low in calories, they provide benefits for the body and brain. Despite its long history, it has only recently been "discovered" as a modern superfood, but in the short time since it was recognized it has received global attention and is fast becoming a household name. This popularity means they are available in most health food stores and even in some supermarkets.

In spite of their tiny size, chia seeds rank as one of the most nutritious foods on the planet. They have loads of fiber, micronutrients, omega-3 fatty acids, and protein. Chia seeds are also loaded with antioxidants; these antioxidants protect the sensitive fats inside the seeds from going rancid. Most of the carbohydrates in chia seeds are fiber. This gives them the ability to absorb 10 to 12 times their weight in water. This can leave you feeling full longer, so they're a great addition to green smoothies when trying to lose weight. They are very high in protein, which is important for muscle repair and appetite control. Chia seeds also have significant amounts of magnesium, phosphorus, and calcium, making them an ideal supplement for bone health, which is essential for young children. Chia seeds have been shown to be beneficial in controlling blood sugar levels by reducing the blood sugar spikes after meals, which makes them a smart choice for diabetics.

Cinnamon: This deliciously fragrant spice is so much more than just a flavor enhancer; it lends itself to a number of important health benefits that keep bodies operating at their peak. Cinnamon helps control blood sugar variations, making it an important spice for children with type 2 diabetes to include in their diets. New research has highlighted the possibility that sugar may be a primary factor that causes cancer cells to thrive, so cinnamon's ability to control blood sugar may hold out new hope for controlling the growth and spread of cancer cells.

Cinnamon is a great option for children suffering from medication-resistant yeast infections. It also works to boost the body's immunity and ability to fight diseases. Cinnamon has powerful antibacterial properties that make it an effective natural treatment for many illnesses. It is especially useful in killing bacteria in the digestive tract, which enables the gastric juices to do their work unencumbered. It helps to reduce bloating and is an effective pain reliever for stomach cramps.

Cinnamon contains high levels of manganese, which is vital for optimal bone health, helps to build strong bones, and is responsible for building and maintaining the connective tissues. Cinnamon has natural calming properties and also helps with mental alertness. This leads to better memory and improved cognition. This spice is ranked as one of the top seven antioxidants in the world, which also helps to ward off cancer by neutralizing the damage caused to cells by free radicals. Cinnamon helps to thin the blood, which effectively improves blood flow around the body. This in turn boosts metabolism and leads to more stable weight.

Cinnamon is also beneficial for fighting tooth decay and gum disease, because of its antibacterial properties. It helps lower cholesterol levels in the blood, which aids heart health. In addition, it contains trace amounts of iron, manganese, and calcium.

While more research is still needed, there are some promising preliminary findings for cinnamon playing a role in the prevention of diseases like Alzheimer's, Parkinson's, brain tumors, and multiple sclerosis. And if all that isn't enough, include it in green smoothies simply because it tastes amazing!

Coconut oil: Coconut oil has many health benefits, ranging from weight loss, stress relief, skin care, and hair care to helping regulate metabolism, aiding digestion, and boosting the immune system. It is also thought to have beneficial properties for those dealing with cancer, HIV, diabetes, high blood pressure, and heart disease. The beneficial properties of coconut oil can be attributed to the caprylic acid, capric acid, and lauric acid it contains. These acids have antibacterial, anti-fungal, antioxidant, antimicrobial, and soothing anti-inflammatory qualities. Specifically, the body converts lauric acid into monolaurin, which helps the immune system deal with viruses and disease-causing bacteria. Capric acid is the same fatty acid found in breast milk. It is a medium chain fatty acid and protects babies from fungal, viral, and bacterial infections. These acids work together as potent fungus and germ killers.

Approximately 90 percent of coconut oil is made up of medium chain fatty acids, also known as triglycerides. Triglycerides are easily digested and go directly to the liver to be used as energy, because of this they are not stored as fat and actually boost the metabolism. Add a spoonful to your kid's green smoothie to give them a super health boost!

Coconut water: This is nature's own energy drink! Coconut water is simply bursting with delicious goodness and is a wonderfully tasty alternative to water. This clear, sweet liquid is composed of a unique combination of vitamins, minerals, electrolytes, amino acids, enzymes, phytohormones, fatty acids, and cytokines. Packed full of nutrients, the following health benefits will help you to understand why it's gaining ground as the world's drink of choice.

Coconut water is naturally low in fat, so you can drink it almost completely guilt free. It's highly beneficial to the skin, because it nourishes it from the inside out. It is incredibly hydrating, so drinking it after bouts of exertion or exercise is highly recommended because it effectively replenishes lost electrolytes and restores the body to a natural state of balance. It is precisely this quality that makes it an effective treatment for stomach bugs that are characterized by excessive diarrhea and vomiting.

Its high fiber content makes it great for digestion. It is also a good source of relief from indigestion and the discomfort associated with acid reflux. Coconut water helps to balance out blood pressure and keep it on an even keel. It contains more calcium, phosphorus, sodium, magnesium, zinc, and potassium than any other drink on the market. Studies conducted on coconut water have shown that it contains significant anticarcinogenic, antithrombotic, and antiaging properties. It is also a rich source of many B complex vitamins, which are essential to good health.

Flaxseed: These tiny seeds pack a powerful nutritional punch. They're just bursting with goodness. Derived from a fiber crop called flax, these seeds are packed full of micronutrients, manganese, vitamin B1, fiber, and the essential fatty acid omega-3. These seeds are a source of healthy fats, which are essential for heart and brain health, as well as being rich in antioxidants, which play a role in lowering the risk of developing diabetes and cancer.

Flaxseed prevents the development and growth of malignant cells in the body by stopping them from being able to attach to the healthy cells in the body. In addition, the lignans in flaxseed prevent tumors from growing, since they disrupt the blood vessels in the tumor and prevent new ones from forming. Without an adequate blood supply the tumor cannot survive.

In order to extract the maximum benefit from these tiny seeds, they should always be ground before consumption, as they can sometimes pass through the digestive system without being digested because they are so tiny. Grinding them releases all that wonderful goodness and primes it to be absorbed by the body. Flaxseeds are very low in sodium and cholesterol, further enhancing the nutritional profile of this much neglected food source. They're also an excellent source of insoluble and soluble fiber. Soluble fiber dissolves in water and helps to keep cholesterol levels and blood sugar levels in check, while insoluble fiber does not dissolve, but helps to sweep toxins out of the digestive system by adding bulk. Getting these little seeds into your diet is crucial, and they're easily incorporated into green smoothies.

Ginger: Ginger is a medicinal treasure trove just bursting with health benefits that have stood the test of time. The Chinese have long espoused the health benefits of this humble root, touting it as a way to cure a myriad of health problems. Ginger is a vital component in the absorption of other nutrients in the body. It's great for nausea or travel sickness, and it helps get the digestive

juices pumping during a meal so the body can effectively digest food and gain the maximum nutrition from it. Great for the digestive system, it helps to calm down bouts of flatulence and bloating, as well as being an effective, natural way to treat stomach cramps.

For centuries ginger has been heralded for its phenomenal anti-inflammatory qualities and is effective at relieving joint pain and soothing sore muscles. Ginger is also a natural decongestant and helps to eliminate nose and throat congestion by loosening up mucus and then gently expelling it, as it is a natural expectorant. Ginger provides the body with energy by improving blood circulation and increasing the base metabolic rate. Rich in magnesium, zinc, and chromium, ginger helps build up the immune system, making it strong enough to naturally ward off colds and flu. It adds a wonderfully deep and spicy flavor dimension to green smoothies, just be sure to use it sparingly for kids until they have developed a taste for it.

Goji berries: Goji berries are a superfood offering more in the way of nutrition than many other foods. Although these berries have only recently gained popularity in the Western world, they have been revered for centuries in the East, where they have been used medicinally and in the culinary arts with huge success. These antioxidant giants help temper the damage caused by free radicals by limiting and reversing the effects of oxidative stress on the body's cells. These berries contain complex starches that help to enhance immune function and fight fatigue. Goji berries contain therapeutic amounts of vitamin A, which helps in the reversal of skin damage, fortifies night vision, and adds an extra boost of support to the immune system. Regularly including goji berries in your diet may also help improve your mood and lessen the symptoms of depression.

They are one of the most protein dense fruits you can find, because they contain all the essential amino acids. They are a rich source of vitamin C, have at least 20 trace minerals, are high in fiber, and contain more carotenoids than any other food. That's a pretty impressive résumé, but that's not all. They have a whopping 15 times the amount of iron found in spinach, making this small berry a true powerhouse of nutrition. This humble berry also contains anti-inflammatory, antifungal, and antibacterial properties, making them a medicinal force to be reckoned with when it comes to fighting infection and disease. This super fruit is a phenomenal addition to any green smoothie!

Green tea: Green tea is more than just tea—it has been dubbed the healthiest thing you can drink because it's loaded with nutrients, minerals, and powerful antioxidants. One of the most important things green tea does is to protect you from the damaging effects of free radicals and strengthening cells to withstand the impact of oxidative stresses; it does this at the cellular and molecular level, literally making you strong from the inside out. It is this antioxidant capacity of green tea that makes it a leading soldier in the fight against cancer by preventing the uncontrolled growth of malignant cells.

Green tea does more than just keep you alert, it also helps to enhance brain function. It contains caffeine, which sharpens concentration and focus, and increases the firing capacity of the neurons in the brain without the jitters that coffee and other stimulants cause. It thus gives you a more stable source of energy, which allows you to be more productive than when you drink lots and lots of coffee.

Green tea also enhances physical performance; it boosts the body's metabolic rate and increases fat-burning potential, as well as injecting you with added energy and stamina. It offers protection from degenerative diseases, such as Alzheimer's and Parkinson's. Green tea has been shown to have antibacterial compounds that reduce the risk of infection and disease. It also kills bacteria in the mouth, helping to prevent tooth decay and strengthening your pearly whites. In addition, it has been shown to reduce the risk of contracting type 2 diabetes, because it naturally regulates the glucose and insulin levels in the blood.

It has been shown to have a positive effect on some of the main risk factors for cardiovascular diseases. In particular, green tea helps lower cholesterol levels. In addition, studies have revealed that drinking green tea can lower the risk of obesity and can help with weight loss, due to the role it plays in boosting metabolism and burning fat.

Hemp seeds: Terming these as seeds is actually a misnomer, as they are surprisingly a fruit! Boasting a sterling nutritional profile, these tiny seeds are something you definitely want to add to green smoothies. They're a great source of protein and contain 10 essential amino acids. These amino acids play a role in mental function and muscle control and help to maintain the cells, muscles, tissues, and organs of the body. These seeds are a pure form of protein that is easily digestible, so the body doesn't need to work as hard to extract the protein. One of the first steps in combatting blood sugar spikes is to eat a high-quality protein. Regular use of hemp seeds will keep blood sugar levels stable by releasing glucagon, which helps keep insulin levels in check. This makes hemp seeds a great food for diabetics to include in their diets. Hemp seeds are also a good source of omega–3 and omega–6 fatty acids, which help protect the brain. They are rich in gamma linolenic acid (GLA), which helps build anti-inflammatory hormones. GLA is important for metabolism and weight loss efforts and helps keep cholesterol levels down.

Hemp seeds are full of phytonutrients and antioxidants, as well as vitamin E, which is good for the skin. They are a rich source of zinc, iron, magnesium, calcium, and phosphorus. Hemp seeds improve blood circulation throughout the body and help stabilize blood pressure. They are an effective aid to digestion, because they are easily digested. With daily consumption of hemp seeds, bowel movements will become more regular and will become synchronized with meals—the benchmark of a healthy digestive system.

Hemp seeds provide a much needed injection of energy that is sustained throughout the day, and the fiber is great for digestive health and helps to keep you feeling full longer, eliminating between-meal snacking. The mild flavor of hemp seeds means they are the perfect addition to your kid's green smoothies, as they blend into the other ingredients unobtrusively.

Maca powder: Maca powder is derived from the maca root, which is part of the radish family. It hails from deep in the Peruvian mountains and has become known as Peruvian ginseng by the local and international communities alike. This root has gained in popularity in recent years as its amazing health benefits have been studied and become better known. While new to most of the world, the benefits of maca have long been held in esteem in its homeland.

One of the most appealing qualities of this root as both a food ingredient and as a supplement is the fact that there are no known side effects related to its use. It has an unusual taste that can take some getting used to; the most common descriptions include "tastes nutty" or "like toasted oats," but when blended with other foods in a green smoothie, it does not have a strong or overpowering flavor.

Maca powder can hold its own nutritionally and boasts a collection of vitamins and minerals that will boost your health. It contains 22 fatty acids and more than 50 natural phytochemicals that are wondrously beneficial. These phytochemicals are critical to hormones, the thyroid, fertility, and the reproductive system, as well as the most important organ in the body, the brain! It is rich in vitamins B, C, and E, and contains iron, magnesium, zinc, calcium, amino acids, and phosphorus.

The iron in maca powder helps to replenish the red blood cells. This directly helps to relieve the symptoms of anemia and indirectly provides protection against cardiovascular disease. One of the main traditional uses for maca powder is for sustained energy and stamina. Users report feeling a natural boost in overall energy just days after starting to include maca powder in their diets. And it is widely used by athletes to help enhance their physical performance.

Maca is also instrumental in building strong and healthy muscles, bones, and teeth, and boosts the body's natural potential for healing. It is used to promote healthy skin, and many swear by its ability to clear blemishes and acne. Maca powder boosts brain function by providing increased focus and clarity of thought, as well as an improved ability to remember and recall information. It also helps to reduce stress and anxiety symptoms and effectively lowers blood pressure.

In addition, it helps regulate blood sugar levels and keeps them on an even keel. It has also been used to improve mood and alleviate symptoms of depression. Maca powder is an excellent supplement for boosting overall immunity and warding off disease-carrying germs.

This miracle food is a must-have ingredient for nutritious, health-boosting green smoothies. Why? Because it works!

Nut and seed butters: These are a good source of healthy fats and proteins, as well as providing some vitamins and minerals, essential components for children's health and growth. They add a creamy texture and a wholesome flavor that is strong enough to mask heavily green smoothies and make them taste fantastic. Try to get organic products if you plan to buy them, otherwise try your hand at making your own.

Pomegranate: This fantastic, sweet, pink fruit—one of the oldest known fruits—originates in Persia and can be found in ancient writings. It is a nutrient-dense fruit that's a rich source of antioxidants. In many cultures and religions, it has been held in high esteem as a symbol of fertility, good health, and longevity. Only the juice and arils of this hardy fruit are edible. Getting the arils out of the tough, leathery outer membrane may seem like an awful lot of effort, but when you see what it offers in terms of overall health, it's well worth the extra effort.

This fruit is rich in antioxidants and phytochemicals, which specifically protect against heart disease and cancer. There is a compound in the pomegranate called punicalagin, which recent studies have shown is especially helpful to the heart. It is responsible for lowering cholesterol levels, as well as reducing blood pressure, and helps clear blockages in the blood vessels of the heart. Lowering blood pressure naturally also helps reduce the risk

of strokes, heart attacks, and other cardiovascular issues. Pomegranate juice improves serotonin levels, which play a role in alleviating the symptoms of depression. It helps to increase bone mass, so it's crucial for growing children, as well as in the prevention of osteoporosis in older people.

The powerful antioxidant capacities of the pomegranate offer invaluable immune support, helping to ward off the germs that cause sickness. In addition, the pomegranate is loaded with vitamin C, so the immune system gets a double whammy of goodness. Pomegranates also contain high amounts of vitamin K, which supports healthy bones, and vitamin B5, which is integral to helping the body to metabolize fats, protein, and carbohydrates.

Pomegranates contain a lot of manganese and potassium, which are instrumental in supporting strong skeletal development and balancing fluid levels at a cellular level. Other important minerals found in this fruit are calcium, zinc, iron, phosphorus, and magnesium.

The pomegranate contains virtually no fat; it does contain some protein and fiber. Pomegranates help with cell regeneration, repairing tissues, helping to heal wounds, and promoting blood circulation to the areas of skin that need healing. Pomegranates help improve skin tone and provide hydration to skin. They also contain enzymes that have antibacterial properties that help keep the digestive system in tip-top shape.

There's a high concentration of iron in pomegranates, which makes it a natural remedy for anemia. Pomegranates are anti-inflammatory, promote blood circulation, and help reduce the occurrence of blood clots. The pomegranate does all this while still fueling the body with energy. This is one fruit that you absolutely cannot afford to exclude from your child's daily diet!

Raw cacao: Chocolate! What kid doesn't like chocolate? While many chocolate products are not healthy for you, it's more about what the cacao has been combined with (usually tons of sugar) than the actual cacao itself. Cacao in its raw state is loaded with some unexpected health benefits. Some of the beneficial minerals in raw cacao are iron, magnesium, potassium, and calcium.

Raw cacao contains a substance called phenethylamine which is a neurotransmitter in the brain that is responsible for elevating the mood, thus cacao is a natural antidepressant. Who can feel sad when they have chocolate in their hand? Raw cacao releases endorphins in the body, providing a euphoric effect that's similar to when you win a prize, exercise, or laugh. It also boosts serotonin levels in the brain, which is the same substance pharmaceutical antidepressants target.

Cacao contains a high percentage of flavonoids, a group of incredibly powerful antioxidants that help fight heart disease and cancer, and may be responsible for slowing down the visible signs of aging. Raw cacao can also help lower cholesterol levels and reduce the risk of developing blood clots. In addition, it lowers blood pressure by increasing blood flow to the arteries, especially those surrounding the heart. The caffeine in raw cacao plays a role in boosting cognitive performance; a word of caution though, consuming raw cacao in excess may not be good for insomniacs due to the caffeine component.

When purchasing raw cacao, look for an organic product, as these have been minimally processed. The commercial brands tend to have a ton of chemicals and sugar in them, as raw cacao can sometimes be a little bitter. That being said, adding a tablespoon of raw cacao to your child's green smoothie, turning it into a "chocolate milkshake," is enough to get even the most resistant child on board!

Turmeric: This Indian spice can be called nothing less than a natural wonder. The health benefits and medicinal properties of this brightly colored spice have taken the world by storm, and now everyone from doctors to dieticians to natural healers are expounding the marvels of this spice. It has antibacterial, and antiseptic properties. It also accelerates the healing and repair of tissues and skin. In particular, clinical trials have yielded promising evidence that turmeric can be beneficial in preventing certain types of cancers.

The popularity of turmeric has increased with the surge in the detoxing craze, as it's a powerful substance to detox the liver. Turmeric removes plaque buildup in the brain, which has a marked impact on the progression of degenerative diseases such as Alzheimer's. Turmeric is also a natural pain killer that has been used effectively in Chinese medicine for centuries. Turmeric aids in the process of metabolizing fat in the body and can play a role in stabilizing weight. In addition, it's a natural anti-inflammatory agent, and as such can relieve the pain and discomfort associated with arthritis.

What to Look for in a Blender

Once your children start to feel the benefits of drinking green smoothies, they won't want to stop drinking them. They're quick, easy, and tasty, and quickly become a part of your children's lifestyle. Once you realize how important green smoothies are in their life, you'll realize just how important it is to have a good blender.

A green smoothie can only be as good as the equipment used to blend it up. Being thrifty when it comes to this piece of machinery only means you'll have to replace it a few months from now when the motor burns out, or paying the price in great heaping spoonfuls of disappointment as bits of fruit pulp clog up a straw or have your three-year-old gagging. Nothing will put an already dubious child off green smoothies faster than pieces of fruit or veggies that have not been properly blended.

To truly appreciate the green smoothie experience, you need a powerful, high-quality blender that can slice through anything in seconds. Unfortunately, those don't come cheap, but a good blender will pay for itself over and over again for years to come. I scoured the Internet and compared many products to compile a list of qualities you should look for when purchasing a blender.

Performance-wise, you should be looking for a blender that meets the following requirements:

- It must be easy to use—no sitting puzzling over instruction manuals, no wondering what all the buttons do—it should embody simplicity!
- It should be efficient and work fairly quickly. You don't want to waste time waiting for the blender to liquefy the ingredients; green smoothie making should not be a chore. You should be able to prepare them quickly with minimal mess and fuss. Your chosen blender needs to reflect this in its abilities.
- Look for a blender that's versatile, one that can liquefy absolutely everything, fruit skins, pith, seeds, ice, everything! Ideally, you want a blender that's multifunctional—one that can blend, chop, churn, pulverize, mix, liquidize, and cream. This helps make the cost a little easier to bear.
- The blender must be able to handle big pieces of fruits and vegetables, so, for example, you can throw in whole bananas. This alone will be a time saver—no more chopping ingredients into tiny pieces before throwing them into the blender.
- You need a tough, durable blender that's built to last. It should have a strong, powerful motor that won't burn out with regular use; in this regard, try to find one that offers some sort of warranty for repairs.
- Some blenders have a built-in cooling fan that prevents the motor from overheating when it's running at high speed. If you can find one that does, it's an added bonus.
- Strong and sharp stainless steel blades that won't rust are also a must. The blades need to be able to slice through ingredients, such as carrots, with ease.
- Look for a blender with different sized smoothie container attachments. That way you can make a small batch for just one or two people, or you can make a large batch for the entire family. These containers should all easily attach and detach; you don't want to be wrestling with a blender at 6:00 a.m.

- If possible, a really nice perk is when the fitted lids have a vent that allows you to add ingredients as the blender is running. This is very convenient, especially when the recipe calls for adding ingredients in stages.
- Look for a blender that stores easily in a cupboard or that is aesthetically pleasing enough to stay out on the counter. Trust me, even the most hard-core green smoothie makers will quickly tire of having to pull out a big, bulky machine and then put it away in the cupboard every time they feel like having a green smoothie. Convenience is key!
- While certainly not an absolute must, look for a blender that does all of the above as quietly as possible. There are many blenders on the market today that operate very quietly considering the ferocity involved in pulverizing the fruits and veggies.
- Last, but certainly not least, you need a blender that's easy to clean. Nobody wants to have to struggle to reach in around the blades after making a green smoothie, where you risk either not cleaning it properly or cutting your hands. Many brands on the market today can be cleaned by adding a few drops of dish soap, filling it part way full with warm water, turning the blender on, and then simply rinsing it out after. This is the feature you want to look for.

Bite the bullet and invest in a great product so you can get serious about green smoothies. Not only will you gain a phenomenal piece of kitchen equipment that will serve you for years to come, but you will have made an investment in the health and wellness of your entire family. That's something you simply can't put a price on.

Tips and Tricks: How to Entice Kids into the World of Green Smoothies

Now that you've made the decision to welcome green smoothies into your life and pitched the idea to the rest of your family, they're suddenly looking at you as if you have sprouted horns. Unfortunately, these kind of health 180s are often not met with the amount of enthusiasm you had hoped. Fortunately, there's lots you can do about that, and I'm here to guide you on the best way to get your family on board and transition your children into drinking green smoothies every day. It's important to note that not all green smoothies are green in color. Many of them are, but a green smoothie really just refers to a smoothie that contains one or more of the green ingredients outlined previously.

Not many kids can resist an ice cold, sweet, ice cream-like treat, and you need to use this in your favor. If your kids are really opposed, start small and gradually work your way up. Add just a few leaves of spinach into their green smoothie to start. As they grow accustomed to the

taste, increase the amount, and then change the type of green you include. Rome wasn't built in a day, and there's no law saying you have to get your kids drinking hard-core green smoothies in any kind of predetermined time frame. The point is to encourage healthier habits and to up their nutrition. Going at it too fast and pushing them too hard may just have the opposite effect. You want to do all you can to encourage them to enjoy green smoothies, and if that means going slowly, then so be it. Better to take longer and get it right, than move too quickly and run the risk that they dig in their heels and refuse to drink them at all.

A great way to start is to make a simple green smoothie, one that contains just a few greens and lots of your children's more favored ingredients, like berries and banana, as a transition. This will help your children become accustomed to the texture and taste without the green color, which, let's be honest, can be a little off-putting. As you take each baby step, add a few more greens and a little less fruit. If you have been adding milk and juices to sweeten them up, gradually reduce the amount of these and add more water. Start with the easy greens first. Things like baby spinach, romaine lettuce, and kale, while packed full of nutrients and vitamins, are fairly

mild in taste. This way you prime your child's palate and get them used to the taste of greens slowly. If you continue this way, soon you'll have a green smoothie lover on your hands: mission accomplished!

If you only follow one rule of green smoothie making, this is it, the pillar upon which all the other rules rest. Without it you are doomed to fail. **Make it Fun!**

That's it, plain, straight up simple, make it fun. Even

the most stubborn child, the leader of the green smoothie rebellion, will be hard-pressed to keep their defenses up if it's fun. Kids of all ages truly love family fun, something the whole family can get involved in. Let's face it, life is busy these days, and there are not as many opportunities for full–on family fun, so when the chance comes along, most kids will grab it with both hands. Play music, sing, and dance while you make green smoothies. Encourage the kids to join in and be as crazy as they like. Then, sit down and talk with your kids about their day or play a game while sipping green smoothies. Let them start associating them with positive family experiences characterized by fun, and you'll see how quickly they learn to love them.

Have green smoothie races. Place a green smoothie in front of each family member, then shout, "On your mark, get set, GO!" Stop half way through and place the glasses next to each other to see who has the lead. Kids will absolutely love this, especially if you occasionally "throw the race" and allow them to win. Kids love these kinds of games, so it's a win-win situation. They get to win the game, and you win because they have gulped down nutrients, vitamins, and goodness without a word of complaint.

Give your green smoothies fun names, such as Shrek, The Green Giant, or The Green Lantern Don't be afraid to be silly. If it makes your kids laugh, they might even ask for that particular green smoothie again, simply because it had a name that stuck in their heads.

Decorate the green smoothies to make them look as appealing as possible. Add twisty straws, bendy straws, umbrellas, flowers, anything that makes them look inviting and draws kids in. You could invest in a glass with your child's favorite character on it and make it the green smoothie glass. You know what will appeal to your kids. When you find something that works, use it.

You can even add something special on top. Whipped coconut cream or dried coconut, or garnish it with a slice of their favorite fruit. Maybe add a sprinkle of chopped nuts, provided there are no allergies. For a very special treat you could add some organic dark chocolate sprinkles. Get as natural a product as possible with a high cocoa percentage: no milk chocolate. In addition, make sure your kids know that it's an occasional treat, not an everyday occurrence. Perhaps a Friday afternoon treat after a long week at school or something special for the weekend.

Most children enjoy smoothies that are made with ice cream. There is a wealth of delicious dairy- and gluten-free ice cream recipes out there, and you could occasionally use these to jazz up

their green smoothies. Ice cream made primarily with coconut or almond milk and fruit is an incredibly healthy addition to green smoothies, and I'll bet your kids won't be able to taste the difference. For these kinds of treats, serve them after meals as dessert. They will have a much thicker consistency, so you can even serve them in a bowl. Labeling it as dessert is a great way to introduce your child to eating healthy treats after meals, and provide them with a few extra servings of fruits and veggies for the day.

Lead by example. You cannot expect your child to sit and sip a green smoothie for breakfast while you tuck into some bacon and eggs or cereal. Young children especially want to copy their parents. If they see you drinking and enjoying green smoothies, they'll be more likely to want to try them too.

One of the most important parts in introducing and assimilating your kids to drinking green smoothies is to explain why. Answer their questions. Don't be the parent who says, "Because I said so," and leave it at that. Nothing makes a kid dig in their heels faster than being presented with yet another set of what they perceive to be imposed restrictions. Explain why you're taking away their usual treats and what the new ones will do for their bodies. Encourage children to seek out information about healthy food choices. The more information you can give them, and the more you can make them understand the reasoning behind such choices, the more you're equipping them to make their own healthy food choices when you're not around. Trust me, this is not as much work as it seems.

Make green smoothies a routine. Decide if it's going to be a breakfast or afternoon snack or dessert. Pick the time of day that's most convenient for your family's schedule and then stick to it. And last, but certainly not least, get your kids involved. Have them help with the prep work, let them throw ingredients into the blender and switch it on, and then let them fill the glasses. On the weekend, when you have a bit more time, let kids create their own green smoothies and experiment with different combinations of ingredients, the more imaginative the better. Few children can resist at least trying something they have made themselves; this is a surefire way to get them excited about green smoothies.

Don't give up—whatever obstacles you face and no matter how hard it seems. Setbacks are to be expected, because children are notoriously unpredictable creatures; what they love today they'll hate tomorrow, and you are bound to meet with a few days of resistance along the way. Studies have shown that adults and children generally accept a new food after a whopping eleven tries, so if your kids don't take to green smoothies straight away, don't despair. Just do your best and don't give in—happy, healthy children are in your sights.

My Child Has Allergies— Now What?

There's no mistaking it, the incidence of food allergies is on the rise. I've heard many people discussing the reason for this sudden surge in food-related allergies, but when you think about it, it's really not all that surprising.

In recent years, scientists have begun recommending that we don the proverbial loincloth and get in touch with our inner caveman if we want to live long and healthy lives. Say what? Yes, you read that correctly, the caveman template for health is the ideal toward which we should all strive. So, what does this mean, and how did scientists reach this conclusion? Let's go right back to the beginning, about 2.5 million years ago.

During this era, man was a nomadic hunter-gatherer. He roamed the earth eating only that which he could kill with a spear or pick off a bush. Why should such a simple and primitive existence be what we strive towards today? Haven't we evolved? The answer is yes and no. Technologically, socially, and industrially we have made huge evolutionary strides, but the fact is that biologically speaking we're still pretty much the same as we were two million years ago. Our bodies really haven't changed that much. Consequently, we're poorly adapted to process many of the foods that make up the modern diet—foods that have become available as a result of our advancements in other areas.

It has been proven that this primitive way of eating is the best way for humans to eat because this is the only diet that complements our genetic make-up, and it is the only diet that will keep us in an optimal state of health. These are pretty hefty claims, but the evidence supports them. When you think back to the cavemen, they were fit, strong, muscular, and agile, with the stamina and endurance to hunt a herd of buffalo for days, the strength to make the kill, and then somehow still have the ability to drag or carry the food back to the cave for the rest of the family. Now look at man today. We are overweight, unfit, stressed, and plagued with a multitude of lifestyle diseases that are slowly killing us. Most of us have trouble climbing a flight of stairs, never mind even coming close to what ancient man could achieve physically.

Scientists have embarked on studies into these ancient civilizations and have discovered that in addition to being in such a peak state of fitness, these societies were also largely disease-free. There were no hospitals, doctors, or medicines millions of years ago, so researchers were led to conclude that diet had to play a major role in the health and longevity characteristic of this era. Moreover, research into modern hunter-gatherer societies garners further support for these claims. There are hunter-gatherer tribes that exist today that follow a diet and lifestyle that's similar to our caveman ancestors, and they too are by and large disease-free peoples. So what went wrong?

The blame can be laid squarely at the feet of the agricultural revolution 10,000 years ago. It was during this time that grains and dairy products came to be included in our diets. These foods were completely new, and our systems had not evolved enough to process them effectively. As a result, our bodies started rejecting these new foods and food allergies were born.

Interestingly, the origins of the "lifestyle diseases" that are so prevalent in our world today can be traced back to roughly 10,000 years ago. There has been a consistently positive correlation between the level of processing our food receives to the number of reported cases of cancer, diabetes, heart disease, Alzheimer's, Parkinson's, infertility, depression, osteoporosis, obesity, allergies, digestive complaints, and the like that plague modern man. In recent years the number of reported cases of these ailments has skyrocketed, which is directly proportionate to the number of fast food chains that have sprung up in every far-flung corner of the globe. Fast food is a booming business, but at what cost? This heavily processed, preservative and additive dense food is not what our bodies need or thrive on. We are engineered to survive on wholesome, natural foods that nourish our bodies and minds.

I am one of a growing revolution of people who unwaveringly maintain that it is the food we eat that is making us so sick. Instead, we should opt for a clean eating regime consisting of lean protein, fruits, vegetables, nuts, seeds, and healthy fats and shun anything processed, such as processed grains, dairy, alcohol, and sugar. The health benefits that have been documented when following this type of diet are numerous. In addition to staving off the major life-threatening diseases mentioned above, when you adopt such a clean way of eating you can expect increased energy and vitality, stable weight, increased muscle mass, glowing skin, healthy hair and nails, an overall feeling of well-being, and no food allergies.

You really can't go wrong with this eating plan—it has literally stood the test of time over millions of years. We all need to get in touch with our evolutionary roots and make a commitment to our health.

With all this in mind, we then wonder why our kids are suffering with allergy symptoms and food intolerances. Fortunately, it can be reversed. By simply cutting out all the contraband you will soon start to see a marked improvement in the symptoms.

Now with regard to green smoothies, I'm sure many of you are scratching your head after my soapbox tirade, after all, a major ingredient in smoothies is milk and yogurt. How do you make a half-way decent green smoothie without these products? Let me say that you do not need them.

I have compiled an extensive list of absolutely amazing green smoothie recipes for you and your kids to try, and milk does not feature in any of them. That's right folks, the recipes in this book are all gluten and dairy free and still tip the scale heavily on the side of yumminess!

However, I do need to point out that many of these recipes do contain nuts, either chopped nuts or nut milks or butters. Don't despair, there are a number of equally delicious substitutions you can use if you have a child who is allergic to nuts. If a recipe calls for one of the nut milks, you can safely substitute coconut milk, coconut water, or plain filtered water. If you're worried about the consistency of the green smoothie, you can add a little coconut cream or avocado to thicken it up. Both are mild enough in taste to not affect the overall flavor.

Avocados and coconut cream are also excellent substitutions for any recipe that calls for one of the nut butters, however, they don't add enough in terms of texture to compensate for a nut butter, especially something as thick and creamy as peanut butter. What I suggest for these recipes is to add some coconut oil or any of the seed butters. Coconut oil adds a fantastic dimension to any green smoothie, as well as a myriad of extra health benefits, but if you're looking for that nutty taste, then a seed butter is the way to go. Both sunflower seeds and sesame seeds (tahini) make delicious butters that will provide that something extra to a green smoothie.

Chopped nuts add a little extra crunch to green smoothies, but these can be replaced. If a recipe calls for chopped nuts, you can substitute in any type of seeds, cacao nibs (for something really special), shredded coconut, or even some oats. A word of caution with oats: oats are naturally gluten free, so they can be safely consumed by those with a gluten allergy, however, many commercially produced oat brands are cross-contaminated with gluten in the factories where they are packaged. Check the label very carefully before purchasing oat products. Ideally, you want to find an organic source of oats where you know there's no danger, especially if your child has a very bad allergy to gluten that will flare up after consuming just a trace.

To make your life easier, I've noted all the relevant substitutions for allergies in each recipe. I hope your children enjoy these green smoothie recipes as much as my children do.

Happy allergy-free blending!

The Lowdown on Sugar, Sugar Substitutes, and Other Sweeteners

The truth is that inside all of us lies an insatiable sugar addict just jonesing for its next fix. That sugar addict is entirely self-created.

I can explain this viewpoint with a simple analogy. Each of us is born with a tiny sugar seed embedded in our body. Every time we eat sugar we fertilize that seed until it is a full-grown sugar monster roaring for more. Think about it, when we try to encourage a baby to take a pacifier or a breastfed baby to take the bottle how many of us have dipped the pacifier or bottle in glucose powder to encourage the baby to suck? When we want to introduce water to a baby, we sweeten it up with juice or a little brown sugar to make it more appealing, and then lessen the amount added until it is pure water. Be honest, how many of you have done this? How many of us reward our children with sweets for good behavior or achievement? I'll bet many of you have uttered the following sentence to your kids at least once: "If you don't eat your dinner, no dessert."

Every time something sweet enters your body that sugar monster smiles and grows a little bigger. Now, don't get me wrong, none of this is done purposefully, it's all born out of the best intentions. The truth is, if you don't give your kids sugar, they can't develop a taste for it, plain and simple.

Besides the taste, sugar has absolutely no redeeming qualities. Take a look at a quick nutritional analysis of a tablespoon of sugar and see for yourself.

1 tablespoon of granulated white sugar:

Serving size, 12 g
Calories, 45
Total fat, 0 g
Cholesterol, 0 mg
Sodium, 0 mg
Potassium, 0 mg
Carbohydrates, 12 g—All sugars, no dietary fiber
Protein, 0 g
No vitamins or minerals at all.

Brown sugar is only marginally better.

1 tablespoon of granulated brown sugar:

Serving size, 9 g
Calories, 34
Total fat, 0 g
Cholesterol, 0 mg
Sodium, 3 mg
Potassium, 12 mg
Carbohydrates, 8.8 g—All sugars, no dietary fiber
Protein: 0 g
No vitamins and only a few trace minerals.

   We happily pump this stuff into our kids with abandon in the form of sweets and desserts. Your average sweet consists of nothing but sugar and a bunch of chemicals, in the form of artificial flavors and colorants, with a bit of gelatin occasionally thrown in for good measure. We let our kids eat all these artificial chemicals and then wonder why things like ADHD, allergies, autism, cancers, and the like are on the rise.
   Fifty years ago diseases and learning problems were rare. Today they have reached epic proportions, with more and more recorded cases every year. I'm not claiming to be any kind of expert, but I would bet my bottom dollar that a large percent of the blame can be laid squarely at the feet of the food we consume. A walk around the grocery store will reveal aisle upon aisle of processed foods, snacks, treats, and sweets, but usually only one or two aisles are dedicated to fresh, wholesome, real foods. That speaks volumes about the society we live in. Even breakfast is no longer just healthy oatmeal. We have Froot Loops, chocolate-coated cereal, and brightly colored grains that look pretty and certainly entice kids to eat them, but what do they contain? Not much in the way of nutrition that's for sure!

Now don't run away with the idea that I'm an earth mother who only feeds her kids foods grown in a little patch of earth in my front garden. Unfortunately, I have made all the above mistakes and learned the hard way, paying the price with my children's health. I decided no more. Was it hard? Absolutely! Do I regret it? Not for a second! All it took were two hard weeks of "detox," a few spectacular tantrums, and a lot of tears behind closed doors from mom. Now I have an eight-year-old who questions if what he's putting in his mouth is healthy, who refuses things offered to him by friends because they are not healthy. My proudest mommy moment came on his birthday, when he refused cake because it would make him sick. His allergies are under control, his moods are stable, and he's doing much better in school now that he's able to sit still and concentrate, much to his teacher's delight.

I'm sure that most of you, if you're reading this book, have also made the decision to be healthy and to get your children's diets cleaned up, but are wondering how to break all the bad habits that have been formed. Well, I'm here to tell you that there is hope. It won't happen over-night, but it can be done. There are other options to satisfy your sweet tooth, because sugar is a vital source of energy and does have a role to play in our body. The crux of the matter is in what form we decide to ingest it.

Eating sweets and desserts spikes our blood sugar levels through the roof, and when they dip again it only makes us crave more sweets to get that same "high" as before. If we make more sensible choices, our blood sugar levels remain on a more even keel and we can avoid the sugar spikes and dips that lead to cravings.

When it comes to green smoothies, I'm the first to admit that some of them definitely need a bit of sweetening. Few of us can chug down a glass of pureed carrots and kale and say we enjoy it without a little something extra, and I would never expect any child to eat what I wouldn't. By all means sweeten your green smoothies, but do so knowledgeably; read the following outline of the best sweeteners vs. the worst ones and why.

Let's start with the taboo ones. These sugars and artificial sweeteners wreak havoc on the body and should be avoided at all costs.

Leading the pack is white table sugar. Why? The answer is plain and simple: it turns to fat! White sugar comes from sugar cane and has been dubbed the cocaine of the food industry.

Highly addictive, it has no place in our diet, period. This rule needs to be applied unwaveringly in your life. If I have to be honest, sugar itself in moderation is probably not the worst thing in the world. The problem with sugar exists because of all the hidden sugars that lurk in places you would never expect them to. As a result, we end up consuming far more sugar than we're even aware of, starting the cycle of addiction. Let me share some shocking stats that will have you cringing. None of these foods are typically deemed to be unhealthy, but after reading these facts their health halos will be forever tarnished.

Bottled barbecue sauce has 2 teaspoons of added sugar per ⅛ cup
Flavored yogurt has 5 teaspoons of added sugar per ¾ cup
Pasta sauce has between 2 and 4 teaspoons of added sugar per ½ cup
Ketchup has 1 ½ teaspoons of added sugar per ⅛ cup
Instant oatmeal has 3 teaspoons of added sugar in 1 packet
Jellies and jams have 1 teaspoon of added sugar per tablespoon
Salad dressings have 2 teaspoons of added sugar per 2 tablespoons
Protein bars have 4 teaspoons of added sugar per bar
And now for the slam dunk, granola, one of the "healthiest" cereals out there, has a whopping
    5 teaspoons of added sugar per cup

Think about this the next time you have a bowl of granola with some yogurt on top for breakfast. Before you congratulate yourself on starting the day with a super healthy breakfast, remember that you have just consumed 10 teaspoons of added sugar! Absolutely crazy, right?

What does this mean for green smoothies when you can't even eat some granola guilt free? It means that you need to be careful when choosing your recipe. When a recipe calls for adding plain sugar, don't. I'm going to provide you with plenty of natural and healthy alternatives. Further avoid the obvious sweeteners, like chocolate syrup, caramel, ice cream, etc. These are loaded with white sugar.

Let me address another gray area of debate when it comes to green smoothies. Many recipes call for prepackaged frozen fruits, which I personally feel should be avoided. When fresh foods are frozen, they may have been frozen before they reached maturity and did not come into their own nutritionally, so to speak. This obviously affects their taste as well. To make them more palatable, sugar is sometimes added, which means when you buy frozen fruits they come loaded with extra hidden sugar. I suggest always using fresh fruits for green smoothies for maximum nutritional value, or to freeze fresh fruit yourself. That way you get the delicious icy coldness that they provide without any of the contraband.

Next on the list is high fructose corn syrup. Most people are aware of this as something to avoid, but what most people don't realize is how omnipresent it is. You need to check food labels very carefully to ensure it's not present in what you consume. Educate yourself; Google is a veritable gold mine of information. You need to be aware of the different names it goes by and know how to recognize if it's in a particular food. High fructose corn syrup is often written on labels as "natural corn sugar." There's nothing natural about it. It is an industrially engineered product that does not occur in a natural state anywhere in nature. It also goes by the monikers isoglucose or glucose-fructose. Avoid it all! High fructose corn syrup is believed to be at the root of the global obesity epidemic and has been flagged as one of the probable leading causes in the sudden spike in diabetes.

Then comes agave syrup, which up until recently has always been considered an acceptable alternative to sweeten foods. Heralded as natural and healthy, it burst onto the health scene amid wonderful reports singing its praises as a sugar substitute and listing all the remarkable health benefits you could expect to enjoy. However, recent research has highlighted that agave syrup may simply have been a product of clever marketing, because as it turns out, it is none of the things it claims to be. Agave syrup is not organic, and it isn't a natural food, and it isn't alive. The natural enzymes are removed from the syrup to stop it from fermenting and turning into tequila.

Agave is actually almost entirely fructose, a highly processed sugar. Sap from the agave plant is extracted and undergoes a fully chemical processing that turns it into hydrolyzed high fructose inulin syrup. (I'm sure I don't need to repeat how bad fructose is for you.) During this process the sap is exposed to heat, and, consequently, the resulting agave syrup is actually devoid of many of the nutrients that are found in the original plant. The process of making agave syrup is not subject to very many quality controls to monitor its production.

There are concerns that due to the shortage of the blue agave plants in Mexico, where most agave syrup comes from, distributors are using inferior quality plants that may even be toxic to keep up with the demand for the product. There have also been concerns that distributors cut the pure agave with corn syrup to make it go further. In what ratios and to what extent this is done is subject to just as much speculation. There have been entire shipments of agave syrup that have been shipped back by the FDA due to the presence of excessive pesticide residue being present in the final product.

Furthermore, agave is not low calorie. Take a look below and see how it compares to regular table sugar:

1 tablespoon agave nectar:

Serving Size: 12 g
Calories: 34
Total Fat: 0 g
Cholesterol: 0 mg
Sodium: 0 mg
Potassium: 0 mg
Carbohydrates: 9.1 g (of which 0.6 g are dietary fiber and 8.6 g are sugars)
Protein: 0 g

Now the media touts agave syrup's most redeeming quality being the fact that it's a low GI source of energy, meaning that it releases its sugars slowly, giving you sustained energy and avoiding the sugar spikes characteristic of regular sugar. However, it seems that not even this is correct. Since agave has anywhere between fifty-five and ninety percent fructose (depending on where the agave comes from and how much heat is used to process it), it's likely to result in the same sort of sugar spikes you would get from consuming regular sugar or high fructose corn syrup.

Fructose is a highly unregulated source of fuel. While the body converts the glucose found in better sugar sources to blood glucose, which is used by the body to provide energy, the liver converts fructose to fat and cholesterol. When the body ingests other sugars, they stimulate the body to produce insulin and leptin, two key factors in regulating and controlling appetite. Fructose, on the other hand, does not, and we lose the natural ability to regulate how much food we eat. In this way, regular consumption of agave syrup can lead to increased food intake and weight gain. So, in conclusion, agave is a highly concentrated sugar that wreaks havoc on your body and health. Its popularity speaks more to a marketing triumph than to any kind of superiority of product.

Last, but certainly not least, on my list of sweeteners to avoid are artificial sweeteners. By pure virtue of the fact that their umbrella term contains the word "artificial," you should avoid them! These come in a myriad of forms, some of the more common ones being sucralose, Splenda, NutraSweet, saccharin, and aspartame. While they can boast of being calorie free, there's no evidence that they help you lose weight. In addition, they are known excitotoxins, which cause damage to the brain, and the plethora of chemicals that these sweeteners contain will damage your organs over time.

Now with all that out of the way you may be scratching your head and asking, "What on earth are we supposed to use then?" Well, the good news is that there are just as many great choices for sweeteners out there that won't do your body any kind of damage if used in moderation. Use any one of the following safe sweeteners in your green smoothies if they need a little "sugar" boost.

The best and easiest way to sweeten any green smoothie is by using delicious, fresh, and juicy fruit. The greater the variety, the better. Fruit is the ideal vehicle from which to obtain the sugar your body needs. This is because the natural sugars in fruit are mostly in the form of fiber, which makes it a slow-release sugar. This slows down the absorption of sugar by preventing the sugar spikes that traditionally accompany sugar consumption. An excellent way to sweeten green smoothies that is often overlooked is to include a couple of dates. Throw them in the blender first and blitz them to a pulp before adding the rest of your ingredients and, voila, naturally sweetened and delicious.

Two more great options, especially for kids, are raw honey and maple syrup. Raw honey has literally been used for hundreds of years as a sweetener. In addition to tasting great, there are a number of amazing health benefits that make it a desirable choice. Loaded with antioxidants, natural enzymes, and an array of minerals such as calcium, iron, zinc, phosphorus, potassium, magnesium, chromium, and copper, raw honey is one of the smartest choices you can make.

Maple syrup also contains an impressive list of vitamins, minerals, and nutritive benefits that make it a healthy choice for sweetening green smoothies. It's good for the heart, boosts the immune system, and improves antioxidant defenses. However, it needs to be mentioned that both raw honey and maple syrup do contain a fair amount of natural sugars and should be consumed in moderation. Ideally, you should find a local, organic source for raw honey and maple syrup. The local farmers' market is likely to have quality products that have been minimally processed.

Some rarer, but perfectly acceptable sweeteners should also be mentioned. You can use organic blackstrap molasses, Sucanat, Lo Han Guo extract, and even coconut nectar to sweeten green smoothies. These ingredients are not as common and would probably require a trip to a specialized health food store, or you can find them online.

If you stick to the guidelines I have outlined for you, your children can enjoy wonderfully sweet and tasty green smoothies without any damage being done to their growing bodies and without feeding that sugar monster! So without further ado, I hope you and your family thoroughly enjoy these recipes.

Green Smoothie Recipes

Beginner Green Smoothies

These recipes are great to ease your kids into drinking green smoothies. The greens are almost undetectable in terms of taste, and these green smoothies rely heavily on the sweet taste to get kids excited about drinking them.

The Banavo

This super simple green smoothie is packed full of all the right things, and it tastes great. The avocado is a perfect source of the right fats, and the banana provides a big boost of potassium. This is the perfect introductory green smoothie.

Yields: 2 Servings

Ingredients:
2 bananas, peeled and cut into chunks
1 avocado, peeled, pitted, and roughly chopped
½–1 cup unsweetened almond milk (substitutions: coconut milk, coconut water, or plain water)
1 tablespoon raw honey (optional)

Directions:
1. Place the bananas and avocado into the blender and puree until smooth and creamy.
2. Add the almond milk slowly until the desired consistency is reached.
3. Add the raw honey and blend again.
4. Serve chilled.

Health Benefits:
- *No cholesterol*
- *Low in sodium*
- *High in vitamins B6 and C*
- *High in dietary fiber*
- *Gluten, dairy, and grain free*
- *High in potassium*
- *Energy boosting*
- *Low GI—balances blood sugar levels*
- *Source of healthy fats*
- *No added sugar*

Serving size: 279 g
Nutritional values per serving: calories, 318; total fat, 20.2 g; cholesterol, 0 mg; sodium, 52 mg; potassium, 952 mg; carbohydrates, 35.8 g; protein, 3.3 g

Tropical Treat Smoothie

There's no other word for this but YUM! Packed full of naturally sweet tropical fruits, even the pickiest of eaters will gulp this down. Rich in potassium and iron, as well as boasting vitamins galore, this green smoothie is set to become a firm favorite.

Yields: 4 Servings

Ingredients:
1 cup baby spinach leaves
2 cups water (divided for steps 1 and 2)
2 bananas, peeled and cut into chunks

1½ cups pineapple, cut into chunks
1½ cups mango, cut into chunks
2 tablespoons diced avocado (optional)

Directions:
1. Blend the spinach and water until smooth.
2. Add everything except the avocado and blend until well combined, adding water to reach the desired consistency.
3. Pour into two glasses and add ice if desired.
4. Top each glass with ½ tablespoon of diced avocado.
5. Serve immediately and enjoy!

Health Benefits:
- *No cholesterol*
- *High in vitamins A, B6, and C*
- *Source of iron*
- *High in potassium*
- *No added sugar*

- *High in dietary fiber*
- *High in manganese*
- *Very low in sodium*
- *Gluten, dairy, grain, and nut free*
- *No added sugar*

Serving Size: 302 g
Nutritional values per serving: calories, 142; total fat, 2.2 g; cholesterol, 0 mg; sodium, 13 mg; potassium, 403 mg; carbohydrates, 31.4 g; protein, 1.6 g

Fruity Fancy Smoothie

This easy green smoothie uses just four ingredients and can literally be ready in minutes. This is a great introductory green smoothie for very young children, as it has apples and bananas in it, which most kids love.

Yields: 1 Serving

Ingredients:
1 apple, cored (peeling is optional)
1 banana, peeled and cut into chunks
½ cup baby spinach leaves
½ tablespoon raw honey
Water as needed

Directions:
1. Throw all ingredients into the blender and blitz until smooth, adding water to achieve the desired consistency.
2. Drink immediately.

Health Benefits:
- *No cholesterol*
- *Very low in saturated fats*
- *High in vitamins A, B6, and C*
- *Very low in sodium*
- *High in dietary fiber and manganese*
- *Source of iron*
- *Gluten, dairy, grain, and nut free*
- *No added sugar*

Serving size: 315 g
Nutritional values per serving: calories, 203; total fat, 0.1 g; cholesterol, 0 mg; sodium, 15 mg; potassium, 701 mg; carbohydrates, 52.6 g; protein, 1.6 g

Manic Mango Smoothie

This is for all the mango lovers out there. This simple green smoothie has just three ingredients, but packs a powerful nutritional punch nonetheless. Add a sprinkle of cinnamon to spice things up a bit.

Yields: 2 Servings

Ingredients:
1 cup kale
Water as needed
2 cups mango, chopped
1 tablespoon raw honey
Cinnamon to taste

Directions:
1. Add the kale and water to the blender and blitz until smooth.
2. Add the mango and raw honey and blend well.
3. Add water slowly until the desired consistency is reached.
4. Finish off with a sprinkle of cinnamon.

Health Benefits:
- *No cholesterol*
- *Very low in saturated fats*
- *High in vitamins A, B6, and C*
- *High in dietary fiber*
- *High in manganese*
- *Very low in sodium*
- *Gluten, dairy, grain, and nut free*
- *No added sugar*

Serving size: 301 g
Nutritional values per serving: calories, 164; total fat, 0.6 g; cholesterol, 0 mg; sodium, 21 mg; potassium, 493 mg; carbohydrates, 39.6 g; protein, 2.1 g

Peary Yummy Smoothie

Pears, good. Bananas, good. Spinach, good. Throw it all together—Exceptional!

Yields: 2 Servings

Ingredients:
2 bananas, peeled and cut into chunks
2 pears, pitted (peeling optional)
1 cup baby spinach leaves
1 tablespoon raw honey
Water as needed

Directions:
1. Throw all ingredients in the blender.
2. Blitz it up.
3. Drink it down.

Health Benefits:
- *No cholesterol*
- *Low in saturated fats*
- *High in potassium and manganese*
- *Low in sodium*
- *Low GI—balances blood sugar levels*
- *High in vitamins A, B6, and C*
- *High in dietary fiber*
- *Gluten, dairy, grain, and nut free*
- *No added sugar*

Serving size: 342 g
Nutritional values per serving: calories, 229; total fat, 0.3 g; cholesterol, 0 mg; sodium, 16 mg; potassium, 755 mg; carbohydrates, 59.8 g; protein, 2.4 g

Sunrise Special Smoothie

This delicious green smoothie will start your kid's day off right, with a powerful boost of vitamins and healthy fats from the avocado. Totally refreshing and clean, the mild flavor of the avocado means you get all the benefits of the fruit with an overriding strawberry flavor. And let's be honest, what kid doesn't love strawberries?

Yields: 2 Servings

Ingredients:

1½ cups strawberries

1 cup apple, peeled, cored, and roughly chopped

1 cup coconut water (substitution: plain water)

1 avocado, peeled, pitted, and roughly chopped

½ cup baby spinach leaves

6–8 ice cubes

1 tablespoon raw honey (or to taste)

Directions:

1. Place all the ingredients into the blender and pulse until smooth, adding more coconut water if necessary to reach the desired consistency.
2. Drink this powerful wake-me-up immediately.

Health Benefits:

- *No cholesterol*
- *High in dietary fiber*
- *Low in sodium*
- *High in vitamins B6 and C*
- *Source of heart-healthy fats*
- *Gluten, dairy, grain, and nut free*
- *No added sugar*

Serving size: 324 g
Nutritional values per serving: calories, 317; total fat, 19.9 g; cholesterol, 0 mg; sodium, 88 mg; potassium, 856 mg; carbohydrates, 33.1 g; protein, 2.7g

Apple Pie Smoothie

Healthy apple pie? Yup, you bet! If this recipe doesn't make a convert out of your kids, then nothing will. Sweet, with just the right amount of spice, this is heaven in a glass.

Yields: 2 Servings

Ingredients:

1 banana

½ cup baby spinach leaves

1 cup unsweetened almond milk (substitutions: coconut milk or water)

½ cup apple puree

1 tablespoon maple syrup

½ teaspoon cinnamon

¼ teaspoon nutmeg

¼ teaspoon allspice

Ice cubes

Directions:

1. Place the banana, spinach leaves, and milk into the blender and blitz until smooth.
2. Add the remaining ingredients and blitz until well combined.
3. Pour into glasses and add an extra sprinkle of cinnamon if desired.
4. Drink and go to heaven.

Health Benefits:

- *No cholesterol*
- *Very low in saturated fat*
- *High in vitamins A, B6, C, and E*
- *Very high in manganese and calcium*
- *High in dietary fiber*
- *Gluten, dairy, and grain free*
- *No added sugar*

Serving size: 225 g

Nutritional values per serving: calories, 111; total fat, 1.4 g; cholesterol, 0 mg; sodium, 98 mg; potassium, 382 mg; carbohydrates, 24.7g; protein, 1.3 g

Amazing Almond Smoothie

This chilled green smoothie has a delicious mild peach and almond flavor. The raw honey adds an enticing sweetness that keeps the kids coming back for more. It's also loaded with all the right stuff to give kids a sustained boost of energy through the day.

Yields: 2 Servings

Ingredients:
1 cup almond milk
½ cup kale
½ cup peach
¼ cup almonds
1 tablespoon raw honey
¼ cup ice

Directions:
1. Place all the ingredients into the blender and blitz until smooth.
2. Pour into glasses and drink up.

Health Benefits:
- *High in vitamins A and C*
- *High in manganese*
- *Very low in sodium*

- *No cholesterol*
- *Gluten, dairy, and grain free*
- *No added sugar*

Serving size: 231 g
Nutritional values per serving: calories, 401; total fat, 34.7 g; cholesterol, 0 mg; sodium, 27 mg; potassium, 571 mg; carbohydrates, 23.6 g; protein, 6.2 g

Pineapple Princess and the Pea Smoothie

The pineapple flavor completely dominates this green smoothie. To counteract the acidity and harshness, banana, pear, and maple syrup have been added. The peas will most likely not even be noticed if this green smoothie is blitzed enough.

Yields: 2 Servings

Ingredients:
1 cup pineapple
¼ cup peas
½ cup banana
½ cup pear
1 tablespoon maple syrup
¼ cup ice

Directions:
1. Place all the ingredients into the blender and blitz until smooth.
2. Pour into glasses and sip slowly.

Health Benefits:

- *Very high in vitamins B6 and C*
- *Very high in manganese*
- *High in dietary fiber*
- *Very low in sodium*

- *Very low in saturated fat*
- *No cholesterol*
- *Gluten, dairy, grain, and nut free*
- *No added sugar*

Serving size: 218 g
Nutritional values per serving: calories, 138; total fat, 0.2 g; cholesterol, 0 mg; sodium, 5 mg; potassium, 337 mg; carbohydrates, 34.9 g; protein, 1.9 g

Berry-Green Smoothie

This vitamin power punch is fit to power a superhero! The blueberries, once sweetened by the raw honey and orange juice, will be an exciting new flavor for the kids to experience. This green smoothie is great for very active children, as it will replenish their systems after strenuous exercise.

Yields: 2 Servings

Ingredients:
¾ cup blueberries
½ cup spinach
¾ cup orange juice
¼ cup banana
1 tablespoon raw honey
¼ cup ice

Directions:
1. Toss all ingredients into the blender and blitz until smooth.
2. Pour into glasses, drink it down, and feel good.

Health Benefits:

- *Very high in vitamins B6 and C*
- *High in vitamin A*
- *High in fiber*
- *Very low in sodium*
- *Very low in saturated fat*
- *No cholesterol*
- *Gluten, dairy, grain, and nut free*
- *No added sugar*

Serving size: 214 g
Nutritional values per serving: calories, 123; total fat, 0.4 g; cholesterol, 0 mg; sodium, 9 mg; potassium, 343 mg; carbohydrates, 30.7 g; protein, 1.5 g

Mango Mayhem Smoothie

Romaine lettuce is quite an amazing plant. It's high in protein, calcium, omega–3s, and iron. It is rich in most of the B vitamins and vitamins A and K. It is also rich in copper, magnesium, manganese, phosphorus, potassium, selenium, and zinc. To top it all off, it has almost no flavor at all, making it the perfect ingredient for those just beginning their green smoothie journey.

Yields: 2 Servings

Ingredients:
1 cup mango
¼ cup romaine lettuce
½ cup banana
½ cup orange juice
¼ cup ice

Directions:
1. Put all ingredients into the blender and blitz until smooth.
2. Serve chilled, drink immediately.

Health Benefits:

- *Very high in vitamins B6 and C*
- *High in vitamin A*
- *High in fiber*
- *Very low in sodium*

- *Very low in saturated fat*
- *No cholesterol*
- *Gluten, dairy, grain, and nut free*
- *No added sugar*

Serving size: 240 g
Nutritional values per serving: calories, 135; total fat, 0.4 g; cholesterol, 0 mg; sodium, 5 mg; potassium, 430 mg; carbohydrates, 32.8 g; protein, 1.4 g

Intermediate Green Smoothies

These green smoothies are perfect for kids who have been drinking green smoothies for a few months and are growing more accustomed to their taste. These recipes rely more on the natural sweetness of fruit than on added sweeteners.

Mint Berry Smoothie

This deliciously simple green smoothie is a sure winner with kids of all ages. Packed full of vitamins, minerals, fiber, and antioxidants, this green smoothie has a delightfully fresh, minty taste.

Yields: 2 Servings

Ingredients:

2 dates, pitted
½ cup baby spinach leaves
¼ cup mint, freshly chopped

¼ cup coconut milk (substitution: water)
1 cup raspberries

Directions:

1. Place the dates into the blender and pulse until they break down and form a paste.
2. Next, add the spinach leaves, mint, and coconut milk. Puree until smooth.
3. Last, add the raspberries and blend again.
4. Pour into glasses over crushed ice to serve.

Health Benefits:

- *No cholesterol*
- *Very high in dietary fiber*
- *Very low in sodium*
- *Very high in vitamin C*
- *High in vitamin A*

- *Nondairy source of calcium*
- *Very high in manganese*
- *Source of antioxidants*
- *Gluten, dairy, grain, and nut free*
- *No added sugar*

Serving size: 171 g
Nutritional values per serving: calories, 158; total fat, 8.0 g; cholesterol, 0 mg; sodium, 15 mg; potassium, 399 mg; carbohydrates, 22.7 g; protein, 2.8 g

Berry Blast Smoothie

Packed full of antioxidant-rich berries, this green smoothie is also full of potassium, iron, and vitamin C and is the perfect way to boost growing bodies.

Yields: 3 Servings

Ingredients:

1 cup baby spinach leaves
Water as needed
1 cup of unsweetened almond milk
    (substitutions: coconut milk or water)
2 bananas, peeled and cut into chunks

½ cup blueberries
½ cup raspberries
½ cup strawberries
¼ cup mint

Directions:

1. Put the spinach and a little water into the blender and pulse until smooth.
2. Add the almond milk and bananas and blend together.
3. Lastly, add the berries and mint and continue to blend until smooth.
4. Serve chilled.

Health Benefits:

- *No cholesterol*
- *Very low in saturated fat*
- *Very low in sodium*
- *Source of iron*
- *High in potassium and manganese*

- *High in dietary fiber*
- *High in vitamins A, B6, and C*
- *Good source of antioxidants*
- *Gluten, dairy, and grain free*
- *No added sugar*

Serving size: 309 g
Nutritional values per serving: calories, 174; total fat, 0.8 g; cholesterol, 0 mg; sodium, 11 mg; potassium, 675 mg; carbohydrates, 42.5 g; protein, 2.8 g

Peanut Butter and "Jelly" Smoothie

This is a healthy take on the classic sandwich filling, using red grapes for the "jelly" and a few dollops of peanut butter. The end result is simply amazing, and kids love it. This green smoothie is loaded with vitamins, minerals, phytonutrients, and antioxidants, so it's not only yummy, it's healthy too. **NOTE: This is not suitable for children with nut allergies.**

Yields: 4 Servings

Ingredients:

1 cup baby spinach leaves

2 cups unsweetened almond milk (substitutions: coconut milk or water)

2 bananas, peeled and cut into chunks

3 cups red grapes

¼ cup smooth peanut butter (omit if allergic to nuts)

Directions:

1. Place the spinach and almond milk into the blender and blend until smooth.
2. Add the remaining ingredients and continue to blend until smooth and creamy.
3. Serve chilled.

Tip: Freeze the grapes overnight to instantly chill this green smoothie. For added crunch, top with some chopped peanuts.

Health Benefits:

- *No cholesterol*
- *Low in sodium*
- *Rich in vitamins B2, B6, C, and K*
- *Low GI—balances the blood sugar levels*
- *High in calcium, manganese, and magnesium*
- *Energy boosting*
- *Gluten, dairy, and grain free*
- *No added sugar*

Serving size: 323 g
Nutritional values per serving: calories, 254; total fat, 9.4 g; cholesterol, 0 mg; sodium, 99 mg; potassium, 668 mg; carbohydrates, 38.4 g; protein, 6.8 g

Sunshine Smoothie

This smoothie reminds me of sunshine, with its golden shades of oranges and yellows. This is a great refreshing breakfast for those hot summer mornings and provides a powerful vitamin boost to start the day.

Yields: 2 Servings

Ingredients:

1 cup baby spinach leaves
1 cup unsweetened almond milk (substitutions: coconut milk or water)
1 cup mango, cut into chunks
1 cup pineapple, cut into chunks

2 tablespoons almond butter (omit if allergic to nuts)
½ teaspoon cinnamon
2 tablespoons oats (optional)

Directions:

1. Put the spinach and almond milk into the blender and pulse until smooth.
2. Add the mango, pineapple, and almond butter and blitz until smooth and creamy.
3. Lastly, add the cinnamon and blend again.
4. Pour into serving glasses and top each glass with a tablespoon of oats if so desired.

Health Benefits:

- *No cholesterol*
- *Low in saturated fats*
- *High in vitamins A, C, and E*
- *Low in sodium*
- *High in calcium and manganese*
- *Source of energy*
- *Low GI—balances blood sugar levels*
- *Gluten, dairy, and grain free*
- *No added sugar*

Serving size: 343 g
Nutritional values per serving: calories, 254; total fat, 11.1 g; cholesterol, 0 mg; sodium, 105 mg; potassium, 562 mg; carbohydrates, 36.2 g; protein, 6.2 g

Popeye Smoothie

Popeye was known for his love of strength-boosting spinach, and your kids will love it too when they taste this delicious blend of ingredients. Full of vitamins, minerals, and antioxidants, this green smoothie is nothing short of amazing!

Yields: 2 Servings

Ingredients:

½ cup fresh blueberries
2 cups baby spinach leaves
1½ cups unsweetened almond milk
    (substitutions: coconut milk or water)

1 ripe banana, peeled and cut into chunks
1 tablespoon raw honey
½ teaspoon ground cinnamon

Directions:

1. Place the berries and spinach leaves into the blender with about half the milk and process until ingredients start to break down.
2. Add the banana and continue to blend until the mixture is smooth.
3. Add the remaining ingredients.
4. Blend until the desired consistency is reached, adding more almond milk if necessary.
5. Pour into large glasses filled with ice.
6. Serve immediately.

Health Benefits:

- *No cholesterol*
- *Very low in saturated fats*
- *Very high in calcium and manganese*
- *High in potassium and dietary fiber*
- *High in vitamins A, B6, C, and E*
- *Source of antioxidants*
- *Gluten, dairy, and grain free*
- *No added sugar*

Serving size: 316 g
Nutritional values per serving: calories, 136; total fat, 2.1 g; cholesterol, 0 mg; sodium, 160 mg; potassium, 542 mg; carbohydrates, 29.6 g; protein, 2.5 g

Festive Smoothie

Why not enjoy the delicious flavors of Christmas all year round? Well, you can with this green smoothie. Cranberries, apples, mint, and cinnamon will have your mind full of yuletide dreams before your glass is empty.

Yields: 2 Servings

Ingredients:

1½ cups fresh cranberries
1 cup coconut water (substitution: plain water)
1 cup apple, peeled and cored
½ cup orange juice, freshly squeezed

¼ cup mint leaves
½ cup romaine lettuce
½ teaspoon cinnamon
Raw honey to taste

Directions:

1. Put all ingredients into the blender and blend until combined.
2. Pour into glasses and enjoy.

Health Benefits:

- *No cholesterol*
- *Very low in saturated fats*
- *High in vitamins B6 and C*
- *High in iron*
- *Very high in dietary fiber*

- *Source of antioxidants*
- *Energy boosting*
- *High in potassium and manganese*
- *Gluten, dairy, grain, and nut free*
- *No added sugar*

Serving Size: 250 g
Nutritional values per serving: calories, 113; total fat, 0.3 g; cholesterol, 0 mg; sodium, 86 mg; potassium, 438 mg; carbohydrates, 24.1 g; protein, 1.1 g

Magenta Madness Smoothie

This bright purple smoothie is aesthetically appealing to children and contains all the goodness of greens from the kale. The berries add a powerful punch of health-boosting antioxidants, as well as a deliciously sweet flavor. Your kids can enjoy this ultimate super food smoothie daily.

Yields: 2 Servings

Ingredients:

1 cup coconut water (substitution: plain water)
½ cup kale
½ cup strawberries
½ cup blueberries

½ cup blackberries
¼ cup beets, steamed to soften
1 tablespoon coconut oil

Directions:
1. Put all ingredients into the blender and blitz until smooth, adding more coconut water if necessary to reach the desired consistency.
2. Pour into a glass of crushed ice and drink.

Health Benefits:

- *Source of antioxidants*
- *Source of energy*
- *Source of heart-healthy fats*
- *No cholesterol*

- *High in manganese and dietary fiber*
- *High in vitamins A, B6, and C*
- *Gluten, dairy, grain, and nut free*
- *No added sugar*

Serving size: 200 g
Nutritional values per serving: calories, 146; total fat, 7.3 g; cholesterol, 0 mg; sodium, 105 mg; potassium, 420 mg; carbohydrates, 16.2 g; protein, 2.0 g

Jungle Juice

This is the perfect after-sport tonic to replenish tired bodies and revitalize sore muscles. The coconut water helps to restore the electrolyte balance in the body, and the watermelon and cucumber help to rehydrate. Cool and refreshing!

Yields: 2 Servings

Ingredients:
2 cups watermelon, cut into chunks
1 cup coconut water
1 cup cucumber, peeled and cubed
1 tablespoon celery, diced

Directions:
1. Place the ingredients into the blender and blitz until smooth.
2. Pour over ice and enjoy!

Health Benefits:
- *No cholesterol*
- *Very low in saturated fats*
- *High in iron*
- *High in magnesium and potassium*
- *Very high in vitamins A, B6, and C*
- *Gluten, dairy, grain, and nut free*
- *No added sugar*

Serving size: 258 g
Nutritional values per serving: calories, 72; total fat, 0.3 g; cholesterol, 0 mg; sodium, 86 mg; potassium, 395 mg; carbohydrates, 13.4 g; protein, 1.2g

Tangerine Twist Smoothie

The fresh citrus flavor of the tangerines combined with the natural sweetness of the raisins make this a flavorful green smoothie. The romaine lettuce is stacked with a variety of vitamins and minerals that make this a super healthy green smoothie.

Yields: 2 Servings

Ingredients:
1 cup tangerines
¼ cup romaine lettuce
¼ cup raisins
½ cup banana
½ cup ice
¼ cup water

Directions:
1. Combine all the ingredients in the blender and blitz until smooth.
2. Pour into a glass and drink. Super easy and super tasty!

Health Benefits:
- *Very high in vitamin C*
- *High in vitamin A*
- *Very low in sodium*
- *Very low in saturated fat*
- *No cholesterol*
- *Gluten, dairy, grain, and nut free*
- *No added sugar*

Serving size: 276 g
Nutritional values per serving: calories, 135; total fat, 0.1 g; cholesterol, 0 mg; sodium, 12 mg; potassium, 446 mg; carbohydrates, 35 g; protein, 1.8 g

P, B, and J Smoothie

This nutritious green smoothie features the jicama, a crunchy root vegetable from Mexico. The jicama root has high quantities of vitamins C and A, and some of the B vitamins. It also contains phosphorus and calcium. It is high in dietary fiber and is also a prebiotic. This green smoothie is an interesting combination of mouthwatering flavors sweetened by the Medjool dates.

Yields: 2 Servings

Ingredients:

½ cup papaya
½ cup blueberries
½ cup jicama

½ cup kale
¼ cup Medjool dates
1 cup freshly squeezed orange juice

Directions:

1. Place all ingredients into the blender and blitz until smooth.
2. Pour into glasses and drink this deliciously sweet smoothie straight away.

Health Benefits:

- *Very high in vitamin C*
- *High in dietary fiber*
- *Very low in sodium*
- *Very low in saturated fat*

- *No cholesterol*
- *Gluten, dairy, grain, and nut free*
- *No added sugar*

Serving size: 253 g
Nutritional values per serving: calories, 184; total fat, 0.5 g; cholesterol, 0 mg; sodium, 5 mg; potassium, 387 mg; carbohydrates, 45.7 g; protein, 2.5 g

Green Immune Supercharger Smoothie

This "super" green smoothie has a kaleidoscope of flavors. It's low in calories, high in vitamins and minerals, high in dietary fiber, and low in fat. It's ideal for all occasions, but especially good for children with the flu, colds, and other illnesses.

Yields: 2 Servings

Ingredients:

¼ cup kale
¼ cup currants
½ cup orange juice

1 cup blackberries
½ cup kiwifruit
½ cup ice

Directions:

1. Place the kale, currants, and orange juice into the blender and blitz until smooth.
2. Add the remaining ingredients and continue to process to the desired consistency, adding more orange juice if needed.
3. Pour into glasses and drink to your health.

Health Benefits:

- *Very high in vitamins A, B6, and C*
- *High in potassium*
- *Very high in manganese*
- *Very high in dietary fiber*
- *Very low in sodium*
- *Very low in saturated fat*
- *No cholesterol*
- *Gluten, dairy, grain, and nut free*
- *No added sugar*

Serving size: 260 g
Nutritional values per serving: calories, 98; total fat, 0.7 g; cholesterol, 0 mg; sodium, 8 mg; potassium, 459 mg; carbohydrates, 22.7 g; protein, 2.4 g

Easy Being Green Smoothie

This is a delicious and highly nutritious green smoothie. The flavor of the cucumber is masked by the sweet and creamy flavors of the other ingredients. It's an ideal breakfast substitute or accompaniment, as it keeps you feeling full and provides sustained energy release. It's guaranteed to be a hit with the kids.

Yields: 2 Servings

Ingredients:
1 cup seedless green grapes
½ cup mango, chopped
½ cup baby spinach
¼ cup cucumber
¼ cup kiwifruit
½ cup almond milk

Directions:
1. Throw everything into the blender and blitz until smooth.
2. Pour into glasses, sip, swallow, and smile!

Health Benefits:
- *Very high in vitamins B6 and C*
- *High in manganese*
- *Low in sodium*
- *No cholesterol*
- *Gluten, dairy, and grain free*
- *No added sugar*

Serving size: 215 g
Nutritional values per serving: calories, 213; total fat, 14.6 g; cholesterol, 0 mg; sodium, 19 mg; potassium, 455 mg; carbohydrates, 22.4 g; protein, 2.1 g

Expert Green Smoothies

These recipes are for kids who are beginning to enjoy the taste of their greens and require less subterfuge to consume them. Since these recipes include more than one type of green, they're tipping the scales more favorably in terms of health and nutrition.

The Green Machine

Three green ingredients make this green smoothie a health powerhouse that kids will love. The coconut oil adds a heart-healthy fat that also aids dental and bone health. Pineapple sweetens it up just enough, but feel free to add a dash of raw honey if desired.

Yields: 4 Servings

Ingredients:

½ cup kale leaves
½ cup butter lettuce
2 cups water
2 cups pineapple, cut into chunks
¼ cup kiwifruit

¼ cup green apple, chopped
¼ cup cucumber, chopped
Squeeze of lemon
2 tablespoons coconut oil

Directions:

1. Blend the kale, butter lettuce, and water until they are smooth.
2. Add the pineapple, kiwifruit, green apple, cucumber, lemon, and coconut oil and blend again.
3. Serve chilled.

Health Benefits:

* *Good source of healthy fats*
* *Good for the heart*
* *Nondairy source of calcium*
* *Strengthens bones and teeth*
* *No cholesterol*
* *Low in sodium*
* *High in vitamins A and C*
* *Very high in manganese*
* *Gluten, dairy, grain, and nut free*
* *No added sugar*

Serving size: 247 g
Nutritional values per serving: calories, 115; total fat, 7.1 g; cholesterol, 0 mg; sodium, 19 mg; potassium, 243 mg; carbohydrates, 14.1 g; protein, 1.6 g

Peachy Keen Smoothie

This green smoothie is delightfully refreshing and packed full of peachy flavor and goodness. Mangoes and apricots add a more complex flavor dimension, but render this a truly phenomenal blend that will be loved by the whole family.

Yields: 2 Servings

<u>Ingredients:</u>

1 peach, peeled, pitted, and chopped
1 mango, peeled, pitted, and chopped
2 apricots, peeled, pitted, and chopped
Water as needed

½ cup kale leaves
1 teaspoon spirulina
1 teaspoon raw honey

<u>Directions:</u>

1. Place the peach, mango, and apricots into the blender with some water and blend until smooth.
2. Add the kale and blend until well combined.
3. Next, add the spirulina, raw honey, and more water if desired and blend together well.
4. Pour into glasses and serve immediately.

<u>**Health Benefits:**</u>

- *No cholesterol*
- *Very low in saturated fats*
- *Very low in sodium*
- *High in dietary fiber*

- *High in vitamins A and C*
- *Energy boosting*
- *Gluten, dairy, grain, and nut free*
- *No added sugar*

Serving size: 241 g
Nutritional values per serving: calories, 119; total fat, 0.5 g; cholesterol, 0 mg; sodium, 3 mg; potassium, 347 mg; carbohydrates, 29.2 g; protein, 1.5 g

Island Delight Smoothie

This green smoothie will make you feel like you're on vacation in the islands. Full of fresh, sweet fruit, it is a delicious after school snack that will replenish and revitalize kids after a long day. The subtle minty undertones make this a truly refreshing drink to enjoy often.

Yields: 4 Servings

Ingredients:

2 cups freshly squeezed orange juice
1 cup pineapple, cut into chunks
1 cup papaya, cut into chunks
1 cup kiwifruit, peeled and roughly chopped
¼ cup baby spinach
¼ cup fresh mint leaves
1 teaspoon spirulina

Directions:
1. Place all ingredients into the blender and process until smooth.
2. Pour into glasses over ice and serve.

Health Benefits:
- *No cholesterol*
- *Very low in saturated fats*
- *Very high in vitamins A, B6, and C*
- *High in iron*
- *High in potassium, manganese, and dietary fiber*
- *Very low in sodium*
- *Gluten, dairy, grain, and nut free*
- *No added sugar*

Serving size: 250 g
Nutritional values per serving: calories, 122; total fat, 0.7 g; cholesterol, 0 mg; sodium, 8 mg; potassium, 523 mg; carbohydrates, 29.2 g; protein, 1.9 g

"The Hulk" Smoothie

Four major greens dominate this recipe and make this green smoothie a force to be reckoned with nutritionally. Sweetened naturally with ripe bananas and dates, this recipe might need additional sweetening due to all the greens. Use a little maple syrup or raw honey if desired. Simple, tasty, and a great way to pump kids full of greens in one easy step.

Yields: 2 Servings

Ingredients:

1½ cups cold water

2 very ripe frozen bananas (the riper they are, the sweeter the taste)

1 cup apple, peeled, cored, and cut into chunks

1 cup baby spinach leaves

¼ cup cucumber

¼ cup chopped carrot

¼ cup parsley

2 tablespoons celery, roughly chopped

1 tablespoon ground flax seeds

2 dates, pitted

¼ teaspoon cinnamon

Maple syrup or raw honey to taste

Directions:

1. Put all ingredients into the blender and blitz until smooth and thoroughly combined.
2. Fill a glass with crushed ice and pour the smoothie in.

Health Benefits:

- No cholesterol
- Very low in saturated fats
- Very low in sodium
- High in dietary fiber, manganese, and potassium
- Source of iron
- High in vitamins A, B6, and C
- Gluten, dairy, grain, and nut free
- No added sugar

Serving size: 392 g
Nutritional values per serving: calories, 184; total fat, 1.2g; cholesterol, 0 mg; sodium, 30 mg; potassium, 711 mg; carbohydrates, 43.1 g; protein, 2.7 g

Krazy Kiwi Smoothie

Kiwifruits are amazing! They taste great and are very versatile. Paired with apples, spinach, and carrots, you end up with a naturally sweet green smoothie that boasts an impressive list of health benefits.

Yields: 2 Servings

Ingredients:
1 cup baby spinach leaves, roughly chopped
1 cup apple, cubed
½ cup romaine lettuce
1 cup unsweetened almond milk (substitutions: coconut milk or water)
4 kiwifruit, peeled and halved
Water as needed

Directions:
1. Put all ingredients into the blender and blitz until smooth, adding water as needed to reach the desired consistency.
2. Pour into glasses and serve immediately for a delicious nutrient boost.

Health Benefits:
- *No cholesterol*
- *Very low in saturated fats*
- *High in dietary fiber and potassium*
- *High in vitamins A, B6, and C*
- *Source of iron*
- *Gluten, dairy, and grain free*
- *No added sugar*

Serving size: 342 g
Nutritional values per serving: calories, 160; total fat, 0.9 g; cholesterol, 0 mg; sodium, 97 mg; potassium, 876 mg; carbohydrates, 37.9 g; protein, 3.2 g

Passion Power Punch

This green smoothie is incredible, so easy to make, yet potently nutritious. This is one for the whole family.

Yields: 4 Servings

Ingredients:

2 cups passion fruit

1 cup orange juice, freshly squeezed

1 cup unsweetened almond milk (substitutions: coconut milk or coconut cream for a thicker smoothie)

1 cup baby spinach leaves

1 teaspoon spirulina

Directions:

1. Put all ingredients into the blender and blend until they are smooth and creamy.
2. Pour into glasses and drink immediately.

Health Benefits:

- *High in vitamins A, B6, and C*
- *No cholesterol*
- *Very low in saturated fats*
- *Very high in dietary fiber*
- *High in iron and potassium*
- *Energy boosting*
- *Gluten, dairy, and grain free*
- *No added sugar*

Serving size: 241 g

Nutritional values per serving: calories, 152; total fat, 1.6 g; cholesterol, 0 mg; sodium, 84 mg; potassium, 577 mg; carbohydrates, 34.3 g; protein, 3.6 g

The Açaí Apple Smoothie

The flavors and natural sweetness of the açaí berries, apple, and banana completely overpower the broccoli in this green smoothie. This one is great for those kids who need to control their weight, as it is very low in calories while still being packed with vitamins.

Yields: 2 Servings

Ingredients:
¼ cup açaí berries
1 cup apple, cored and peeled
¼ cup broccoli florets, sliced and frozen
½ cup kale
¼ cup carrots
½ cup banana
½ cup ice

Directions:
1. Throw everything into the blender and blitz until smooth.
2. Serve chilled.

Health Benefits:
- *Very high in vitamins A, B6, and C*
- *High in dietary fiber*
- *Low in sodium*
- *Very low in saturated fat*
- *No cholesterol*
- *Gluten, dairy, grain, and nut free*
- *No added sugar*

Serving size: 205 g
Nutritional values per serving: calories, 119; total fat, 0 g; cholesterol, 0 mg; sodium, 43 mg; potassium, 281 mg; carbohydrates, 18.3 g; protein, 11.7 g

L.G.M. Smoothie

Cucumbers are rich in phytochemicals, among other things. Phytochemicals are plant antibacterials that help fight unwanted bacteria in our bodies. Romaine lettuce is known for providing a wide variety of vitamins and minerals. This green smoothie will give your kids the power to fight off any "little green men" that may try to cause illness.

Yields: 2 Servings

Ingredients:
½ cup romaine lettuce
½ cup guava juice
½ cup mango juice
½ cup cucumber
½ cup banana
½ cup kiwifruit

Directions:
1. Combine all ingredients in the blender and blitz until smooth.
2. Pour into glasses over ice and serve with a straw. Feel the bugs getting blasted!

Health Benefits:
- *Very high in vitamins B6 and C*
- *High in potassium*
- *High in dietary fiber*
- *Very low in sodium*
- *Very low in saturated fat*
- *No cholesterol*
- *Gluten, dairy, grain, and nut free*
- *No added sugar*

Serving size: 188 g
Nutritional values per serving: calories, 102; total fat, 0.7 g; cholesterol, 0 mg; sodium, 4 mg; potassium, 502 mg; carbohydrates, 24 g; protein, 2.2 g

Three Berry Green Smoothie

This is a well-balanced, all-around good green smoothie. All the ingredients are loaded with vitamins and good nutrition. It has a nice calorie count to ensure that the drinker has enough energy to keep them going and a good amount of fiber to keep them feeling satiated longer.

Yields: 2 Servings

Ingredients:

¼ cup blueberries
¼ cup raspberries
¼ cup strawberries
½ cup kale

½ cup avocado
½ cup orange juice
1 teaspoon spirulina
½ cup ice

Directions:
1. Toss all ingredients into the blender and blitz until smooth.
2. Drink and enjoy!

Health Benefits:
- *Very high in vitamins A, B6, and C*
- *High in manganese*
- *High in dietary fiber*
- *Very low in sodium*
- *No cholesterol*
- *Gluten, dairy, grain, and nut free*
- *No added sugar*

Serving size: 195 g
Nutritional values per serving: calories, 121; total fat, 7.4 g; cholesterol, 0 mg; sodium, 12 mg; potassium, 387 mg; carbohydrates, 14 g; protein, 1.8 g

Pompous Pom Smoothie

Celery is an excellent detoxifier for the body. It helps the kidneys flush toxins and helps the body deal with stress on all levels. The kale is a superfood, filled with vitamins and minerals. The pomegranate, strawberries, and banana round out a delectable fruity taste that kids will love.

Yields: 2 Servings

Ingredients:
½ cup kale
½ cup celery, chopped
½ cup pomegranate juice
1 cup banana
½ cup strawberries

Directions:
1. Put the kale, celery, and pomegranate juice into the blender and process until smooth.
2. Add the banana and strawberries and continue to blitz.
3. Pour, drink, and be merry!

Health Benefits:

- *Very high in vitamins A, B6, and C*
- *High in potassium*
- *High in manganese*
- *High in dietary fiber*
- *Low in sodium*
- *Very low in saturated fat*
- *No cholesterol*
- *Gluten, dairy, grain, and nut free*
- *No added sugar*

Serving size: 215 g
Nutritional values per serving: calories, 129; total fat, 0.2 g; cholesterol, 0 mg; sodium, 35 mg; potassium, 636 mg; carbohydrates, 31.9 g; protein, 1.7 g

Greenland Smoothie

Mint provides a healthy dose of vitamin A, which promotes healthy skin and support for the immune system. The baby spinach gives a kick of brain-healthy antioxidants and iron. The avocado provides a significant dose of vitamin E, and the kiwifruit ups the fiber quotient.

Yields: 2 Servings

Ingredients:

1 cup ice
¼ cup baby spinach
¼ cup cucumber
¼ cup avocado

¼ cup kiwifruit
½ cup orange juice
1 tablespoon parsley, chopped
¼ cup mint leaves

Directions:
1. Place all ingredients in the blender and blitz until smooth.
2. Pour into glasses, drink this green machine smoothie, and feel great!

Health Benefits:
- *Very high in vitamins B6 and C*
- *High in vitamins A and E*
- *High in iron*
- *High in dietary fiber*

- *Very low in sodium*
- *No cholesterol*
- *Gluten, dairy, grain, and nut free*
- *No added sugar*

Serving size: 249 g
Nutritional values per serving: calories, 87; total fat, 3.9 g; cholesterol, 0 mg; sodium, 12 mg; potassium, 375 mg; carbohydrates, 12.8 g; protein, 1.6 g

Lemonade Smoothie

This luscious lemony green smoothie has just the right blend of goodness and taste to satisfy kids. The lemon is delightfully refreshing, and the tartness is counteracted by the sweetness of the orange and apple. The broccoli and celery, in addition to the vitamin and mineral boost, provide an injection of greens that elevates this green smoothie to health bomb status.

Yields: 2 Servings

Ingredients:
1 cup orange juice, freshly squeezed
½ cup lemon juice
¼ cup broccoli
¼ cup celery
1 cup apple
Water as needed

Directions:
1. Place all ingredients in the blender and blitz until smooth.
2. Drink it chilled.

Health Benefits:
- *Very high in vitamins B6 and C*
- *High in potassium*
- *High in dietary fiber*
- *Low in sodium*
- *No cholesterol*
- *Gluten, dairy, grain, and nut free*
- *No added sugar*

Serving size: 232 g
Nutritional values per serving: calories, 91; total fat, 0.7 g; cholesterol, 0 mg; sodium, 28 mg; potassium, 371 mg; carbohydrates, 20.6 g; protein, 1.8 g

Conclusion

That's it folks, the complete guide to green smoothies for your kids. You now have all the knowledge you need in your arsenal to raise happy, healthy, green smoothie loving kids!

As long as you remember the golden rule of green smoothies—make it fun—you can't go wrong. Education is key, and in this regard this guide will set you up on your green smoothie journey. However, never stop seeking new information, and continue to make yourself knowledgeable on all aspects of your children's health. There's groundbreaking research emerging all the time about the health benefits of little known foods; make sure you stay up to date so you'll always know how to pack green smoothies full of the purest form of nutrition with a massive health benefit "bomb" as your secret ingredient!

Keep searching for new and better combinations of ingredients. As long as you know the basics about what different ingredients can do for your child's body, there are no hard and fast rules to green smoothie blending; it truly is a subjective culinary art.

So, what are you waiting for? Get your family to the store, pick out your equipment and ingredients, and get into the kitchen for some healthy family fun! I hope you enjoy the recipes I have chosen for you, they really are delicious and nutritious. Feel free to tweak the ingredients in the recipes to suit your children's needs and tastes.

And, finally, say goodbye to your kids feeling sluggish and unhealthy and welcome in the era of healthy, vibrant kids!

Index